BRIEF STRATEGIC INTERVENTION FOR SCHOOL BEHAVIOR PROBLEMS

BRIEF STRATEGIC INTERVENTION FOR SCHOOL BEHAVIOR PROBLEMS

Ellen S. Amatea

Jossey-Bass Publishers

San Francisco • London • 1989

BRIEF STRATEGIC INTERVENTION FOR SCHOOL BEHAVIOR PROBLEMS
by Ellen S. Amatea

Copyright © 1989 by: Jossey-Bass Inc., Publishers
350 Sansome Street
San Francisco, California 94104

&

Jossey-Bass Limited
28 Banner Street
London EC1Y 8QE

Figures 1 and 2 and excerpts in Chapters Two and Four are
reprinted from *CHANGE: Principles of Problem Formation and
Problem Resolution*, by Paul Watzlawick, John H. Weakland, and
Richard Fisch, by permission of W. W. Norton & Company, Inc.
Copyright © 1974 by W. W. Norton & Company, Inc.

Library of Congress Cataloging-in-Publication Data

Amatea, Ellen S., date.
  Brief strategic intervention for school behavior problems / Ellen
S. Amatea. — 1st. ed.
      p.   cm. — (A Joint publication in the Jossey-Bass social and
behavioral science series and the Jossey-Bass education series)
    Bibliography: p.
    Includes index.
    ISBN 1-55542-174-1 (alk. paper)
    1. Problem children—Education—United States.   2. Behavior
modification—United States.   I. Title.   II. Series: Jossey-Bass
social and behavioral science series.   III. Series: Jossey-Bass
education series.
LC4801.5.A48   1989
371.93—dc20

Manufactured in the United States of America

JACKET DESIGN BY WILLI BAUM
FIRST EDITION

Code 8948

A joint publication in

**The Jossey-Bass
Social and Behavioral Science Series**

and

The Jossey-Bass Education Series

Consulting Editors
Psychoeducational Interventions:
Guidebooks for School Practitioners

Charles A. Maher
Rutgers University

Joseph E. Zins
University of Cincinnati

CONTENTS

ix

PREFACE

Brief Strategic Intervention for School Behavior Problems has been written for school helping professionals—specifically, school counselors, school psychologists, and school social workers. These professionals often must consider using more intensive therapeutic strategies when student problems do not respond to simple corrective action such as providing support, requesting a change in behavior, or using behavioral conditioning. The student, for example, who refuses to attend school, is afraid to eat or mix with other children, or openly resists his teacher's direction may require intensive therapeutic action. When such situations arise, individual child or family counseling approaches are often considered. However, these familiar intervention approaches require long-term commitments of time and energy in addition to the involvement of a sizable number of non-school persons (for example, members of the student's family). Because school helping professionals need to limit the amount of time and energy they devote to any one student case so that they can serve all their clients, they often encounter difficulty using these more intensive counseling approaches within the school setting.

Note: Rather than use the awkward "he or she" and "him or her" throughout the book, as no inclusive pronoun has been generally adopted, I have in some instances varied the gender of the pronoun, thus giving approximately equal attention to female and male.

Now, however, a newly developing mode of brief, problem-oriented intervention has begun to find its way into school practice. Because this intervention approach assumes that efforts to solve persistent student problems (that is, problems that do not respond to direct behavioral interventions) can be effective within a limited time frame, it is particularly appealing to school helping professionals, who previously had few options available for working with students whose problems seemed resistant to simple corrective actions.

This approach, known variously as brief strategic intervention, brief strategic therapy, or brief family therapy, is based on the brief therapy model developed by Paul Watzlawick, John Weakland, and Richard Fisch of the Brief Therapy Center of the Mental Research Institute (MRI) in Palo Alto, California. These men have generated a number of important publications that have defined and elaborated on the meaning of brief strategic therapy. Their book *Change: Principles of Problem Formation and Problem Resolution* (Watzlawick, Weakland, and Fisch, 1974) provides an explicit statement of the theory supporting this approach, while a subsequent book, *The Tactics of Change* (Fisch, Weakland, and Segal, 1982), describes the techniques and methods used.

Unfortunately, these books, along with most other published reports describing the MRI brief therapy model, have focused only on how non-school mental health professionals have applied this model. This is a regrettable oversight, since the school is often heavily involved in attempting to resolve a student's problem. Consequently, in this book I illustrate how the ideas and methods of brief strategic intervention can be applied in the schools. Because my colleagues and I have found ourselves achieving some remarkably successful results in the schools with students whose problems had not responded to simpler interventions, we realize this approach can be quite useful to school helping professionals. This book describes our efforts to extend the brief strategic approach proposed by MRI to the school setting. It is based on my twelve years of experience teaching family systems therapy to school helping professionals and other mental health professionals and thus represents an adaptation of the best ideas and methods of family systems therapy to the context of the school.

Overview of the Contents

Brief Strategic Intervention for School Behavior Problems is divided into four parts. Part One discusses the distinctive premises about the nature of human problems and their resolution on which this approach is based. Chapter One describes, using an actual case study, the characteristic manner in which problems are conceptualized and resolved and then contrasts this with the behavioral and strategic family counseling approaches familiar to many school practitioners. Chapter Two explains how these premises are translated into specific intervention procedures and outlines the general sequence of stages comprising this intervention process.

Part Two, consisting of Chapters Three through Eight, describes in detail how the intervention process is carried out. Chapter Three discusses how one goes about deciding when to use brief strategic intervention tactics—obviously, no intervention approach is appropriate for all situations. This chapter considers problem contexts for which brief strategic intervention is and is not appropriate. Chapter Four addresses the general issue of the school practitioner's control over the intervention process, with emphasis on the issues that commonly arise early on and shape the amount of influence she can have. This topic is placed early in the text because often the practitioner can lose control over the intervention process either during the initial contact regarding a student or in early meetings with him. Chapter Five describes the kinds of information that are needed to resolve student problems briefly. In addition, methods for collecting this information are considered. Chapter Six gives special emphasis to gathering information about those client beliefs that are central to maintenance (and thus to resolution) of a student's problem. This information is essential for the practitioner to have if she is to foster the student's compliance with her intervention directives and avoid problems with resistance. Chapter Seven describes how this information is used to formulate specific tactics to resolve the problem. Finally, Chapter Eight addresses the common issues that arise in planning a monitoring and evaluation strategy.

The first three chapters in Part Three illustrate the actual process of implementing this approach within the school. Three different case studies are reported. Each case shows helping professionals working with a student demonstrating problems at school. (Of course, all names and information leading to the identity of the actual persons involved have been carefully disguised to protect these individuals' anonymity.) In each of these chapters, extensive excerpts of case dialogue are included, along with records of the thinking of the school professional as to why particular moves were made. This is done so that the reader can see how the package of intervention steps comes together in practice. Finally, Chapter Twelve discusses issues concerning ethical use of these intervention methods.

You will note that the terms *client, problem person,* and *problem-bearer* are used more or less interchangeably throughout the book to refer to the person or persons with whom the school practitioner works. In addition, I sometimes refer to the *counselor, psychologist,* or *social worker* but more often use the term *practitioner* or *helping professional* to encompass these varied professionals. You will also note that in some of the cases presented I was the helping professional. In the majority of cases, however, I was the supervisor of school mental health professionals in pre-service and in-service training programs in which I worked with them to plan and carry out the intervention.

Acknowledgments

The Counselor Education Department at the University of Florida in Gainesville, Florida, in which I have taught for the past fourteen years, has afforded me a wonderful opportunity to experiment with different ways of resolving students' school problems and teaching school helping professionals how to apply these methods. The school helping professionals who conducted the cases presented in this book were in various positions in the schools. Some, such as Lynette Lockhausen and Patricia Carrow, were in training as school psychologists, school counselors, or family therapists. Others, such as Margaret Cuthbert and Cynthia Cummings, were professionals already out in the schools. Each taught me as I taught them. I am indebted to them all for contributing to the development of the ideas expressed in this book and especially to Patricia Carrow for her contribution in writing Chapter Eleven.

I am also indebted to Joseph Wittmer, my chairperson in the Counselor Education Department at the University of Florida, who provided an atmosphere in which new ideas and creative approaches to counseling and counselor training have flourished—and who encouraged me to write this book. I particularly appreciate the help of Gail Cross, Linda Foy, Robert Myrick, Peter Sherrard, and John Weakland, who kindly read portions of the manuscript and suggested improvements. Charles A. Maher and Joseph E. Zins, consulting editors for Jossey-Bass's series on psychoeducational interventions, also helped considerably, giving generously of their time to several careful readings of the manuscript and being calm and considerate throughout the final stages of preparation. Gracia Alkema also has my sincere thanks in encouraging the development of this book in its final form and shepherding it over all the technical hurdles. Finally, I am particularly grateful to my husband, Frank Amatea, without whose support, encouragement, and help this book would not have been written, and to my mother, Vivian Sherlock, who read, edited, and supported all the early drafts of this book and never failed to give me the definitive praise and critiques I needed.

Four chapters in this work have been published elsewhere in somewhat different form. A portion of Chapter One, "Brief Strategic Intervention: A New Alternative," was published under the title "Brief Strategic Intervention: A New Approach to School Counseling Practice" and appeared in the *Elementary School Guidance and Counseling Journal* (Amatea and Lockhausen, 1988). A portion of Chapter Four, "Managing the Change Process," was published under the title "Engaging the Reluctant Client: Some New Strategies for the School Counselor" and appeared in *The School Counselor* (Amatea, 1988b). Portions of Chapter Seven appeared in an article entitled "Reversing the School's Response: A New Approach to Resolving Persistent School Problems" in the *American Journal of Family Therapy* (Amatea and Sherrard, 1989). Finally, Chapter Nine, "A Case of Persistent Temper Tantrums," was published in different form under the title "Brief Systemic Intervention: A Case of Temper Tantrums" and appeared in *Psychology in the Schools* (Amatea, 1988a).

Ocala, Florida   Ellen S. Amatea
August 1989

THE AUTHOR

Ellen S. Amatea, a clinical member of the American Association for Marriage and Family Therapy, received her B.S. degree (1964) from Colorado State University in psychology and both her M.S. degree (1966) in guidance and counseling and her Ph.D. degree (1972) in counselor education from Florida State University. Currently she is an associate professor of counselor education at the University of Florida, where, since 1975, she has been a member of the school counseling and counseling psychology graduate training faculty. She has authored numerous articles on the application of family systems concepts and techniques in the school setting, which have appeared in various school counseling, school psychology, and family therapy journals.

**BRIEF STRATEGIC INTERVENTION
FOR SCHOOL BEHAVIOR PROBLEMS**

PART ONE

Handling Problem Behaviors in Schools

A new set of very promising ideas and methods has begun to find its way into the area of psychoeducational intervention in the schools. Variously known as brief therapy, brief family therapy, or brief strategic intervention, this approach is based on a view of psychological problems and their resolution that is radically different from most established modes of child-focused psychological treatment. Originally developed by mental health professionals as a method for shortening the process of treating severe psychological problems, this approach evolved unexpectedly into a new way of looking at human problems and resolving them in a brief time.

In this approach, developed by Paul Watzlawick, John Weakland, and Richard Fisch of the Brief Therapy Center of the Mental Research Institute (MRI), human problems are viewed as interactional and nonpathological. Thus, problem behaviors are viewed in relation to their wider, ongoing social contexts (for example, a student's home or school) rather than in isolation within the individual. However, in contrast to traditional family therapy, which attempts to modify underlying family relationships, practitioners of brief strategic intervention only target key interactional patterns around the problem behavior for change. In doing this, the practitioner typically gives explicit attention to influencing people to stop nonproductive patterns of interaction and start more productive ones in as brief a time as possible.

Because this intervention approach assumes that effective interventions in persistent psychological problems can occur within a limited time, it has been particularly appealing to school helping professionals (that is, school counselors, psychologists, and social workers), who previously had few options for working with students whose problems seemed resistant to simple corrective actions. For unlike traditional models of child and family intervention, in which short-term interventions are viewed as shortcuts, this approach does not assume that a significant amount of time and effort must be committed to changing the student.

But what is brief strategic intervention? How does it differ from other, more familiar models of child-focused intervention? Are there some cases to which it applies and others to which it does not? Up until now, there have been few sources of information on the use of brief strategic intervention in the schools. Instead, most of the available literature has discussed the use of this approach only with the families of individuals experiencing psychological problems. This book addresses that problem by illustrating how this intervention approach can be applied by the school helping professional. Part One, consisting of Chapters One and Two, describes the brief strategic approach and explains the premises on which it is based. In Chapter One, the approach is described and contrasted with two intervention approaches familiar to most school helping professionals—behavior therapy and strategic family therapy. In Chapter Two, the major premises on which this approach is based are described in detail, with emphasis on problem definition and resolution.

CHAPTER 1

Brief Strategic Intervention: A New Alternative

Mrs. Folsom, the school lunchroom aide, and a plump, third-grade girl named Niki are standing in the doorway of the school counselor's office looking noticeably upset. As the counselor invites them in, Mrs. Folsom says, "I don't know what to do about Niki. This is the third time this week she has vomited in the lunchroom! I don't know what is the matter. She never eats all of the food on her tray, even after we've told her she needs to eat a good lunch. We've tried to be understanding, but she's just got to stop doing this!" Niki, looking embarrassed as Mrs. Folsom speaks, says nothing. Sensing the child's reluctance to speak, the counselor thanks the lunchroom aide for bringing Niki to her, suggests the aide leave so she might talk further with Niki, and then invites Niki to talk.

Counselor: Niki, you look unhappy.

Niki: (Answers with only a nod of her head, eyes downcast.)

Counselor: I know you have been sick in the cafeteria, and I want to help you, so I hope you will tell me what happened in the lunchroom today just before you threw up.

Note: This chapter is an expanded and revised version of an article, entitled "Brief Strategic Intervention: A New Approach to School Counseling Practice," coauthored by Lynette Lockhausen (published in the *Elementary School Guidance and Counseling Journal*, 1988, 22, 39–47). It is reprinted here with her permission and with the permission of AACD Publications.

Niki: Well, I was sitting with my friends at the table, looking at all the food in front of me. I don't like it all, but I knew somebody would tell me to eat it all. I watched the other girls eat, and I started to feel sick. Then Mrs. Folsom came by and put her hand on my shoulder. She said, "Quit dawdling, honey, and eat your good lunch." She helps cook the lunches, so she thinks they're real good. I tried to eat, but I felt sicker and sicker. Then I threw up.

Counselor: What happened then?

Niki: All of the girls moved away, and one of them went to get Mrs. Folsom, and another went to get the janitor. Nobody was happy, especially me, but I just couldn't help it—I never can!

Counselor: It's scary when you feel sick and you think you are going to throw up. I wonder if there are other times when you feel that way.

Niki: How did you know? I always feel sick in my bed at night, and now I'm starting to feel sick in my classroom.

Counselor: How about the classroom? What happens there?

Niki: Mrs. Paulie is a nice teacher, but she gets busy with the other kids. I start to feel sick and raise my hand to tell her. When she doesn't see me, I feel sicker and sicker until I throw up.

Counselor: You are helping me to understand, Niki. Thank you. Now tell me about feeling sick at home in your bed. Start by telling me what usually happens right after you get off the school bus in the afternoon.

Niki: Well, I go home and see my mama. I tell her what I learned at school. Then she starts dressing for work, and I go play with my friends. Then I say goodbye to mama.

Counselor: So your mama works at night? When did your mama get her night job?

Niki: About two weeks ago. Before that, we ate dinner together.

Counselor: What happens after playing with your friends, Niki?

Niki: My aunt calls me to eat dinner with my cousins. She takes care of me when my mama is at work. She's so grouchy. She fills my plate full of food—much more than my cousins—then she says I have to eat it all. I start eating. Then I get full, but she says I have to sit there until I finish. When I finally finish, I go to bed.

Counselor: Is that a new rule—to finish your food even when you are full?

Niki: It's my aunt's rule. My mama never makes me do that.

Counselor: When you are in your bed, what happens?

Niki: I think about all that food that only I had to eat, and I feel sicker and sicker until I throw up. Then I go to sleep. Then my mama gets home in the night and wakes me up and cleans me and my bed. I feel better then, and I go back to sleep until morning.

The intervention that began with this exchange was the beginning of a radically different approach to the problem of Niki's vomiting. Instead of focusing on Niki's feelings and attitudes or on the pattern of school or family relationships in which Niki was involved, the counselor chose to examine the specific sequence of actions and reactions in which Niki's vomiting behavior was embedded. By questioning Niki as to what exactly happened when she vomited, who was involved, and how they responded, the counselor found out more about the problem situation and how it was being handled. But why do this?

This was the first step in using brief strategic intervention, a newly developing approach designed to resolve Niki's problem in a brief amount of time. Because of its short-term focus, this approach is particularly appealing to school helping professionals, who typically have limited time to devote to any one student. Since traditional child and family counseling approaches require large amounts of time to change student behavior, they have been poorly suited to use in the schools. For example, if the counselor had decided to use a Rogerian approach to counsel Niki, exploring the girl's thoughts and feelings about her present life and the people in it, she would have had to commit a significant amount of time to this effort. Or if the counselor had decided to employ a family systems approach, observing and restructuring relationships between Niki and her family, her approach would also have taken a significant amount of time. Now, however, brief strategic intervention gives counselors a new option. Unlike traditional models of child and family counseling practice, in which short-term interventions are viewed as shortcuts, this mode assumes that effective intervention in solving persistent student problems can occur in a limited time.

Brief strategic intervention, in other words, represents a major departure from familiar ways of thinking about and working with students and their problems. Growing out of some twenty years of clinical research and experimentation conducted at MRI's Brief Therapy Center by Paul Watzlawick, John Weakland, and Richard Fisch, it represents an important new short-term approach for working with children and adolescents demonstrating persistent problems at school.

Interestingly, the work at the Brief Therapy Project began merely as an investigation of treatment with people of all ages in which innovative techniques were employed to shorten the treatment process. However, the project evolved unexpectedly into a new way of viewing human problems and intervening to solve those problems. A number of reports have appeared in the family therapy literature (Fisch, 1977; Fisch, Weakland, and Segal, 1982; Watzlawick, Weakland, and Fisch, 1974; Weakland, Fisch, Watzlawick, and Bodin, 1974; Weakland, 1977b) describing how this approach has been used to resolve children's and adolescents' problematic behavior. Only recently, however, has this approach begun to be used at school with students demonstrating common school behavior or achievement problems (Amatea, 1988a; Amatea and Lockhausen, 1988; Kral, 1986; Williams and Weeks, 1984; Wiswell, 1986).

To introduce you to this new intervention approach, let us return to the school counselor and Niki. Instead of thinking of Niki's vomiting as resulting from some individual emotional state or as serving some function within Niki's family, the counselor viewed Niki's vomiting as being triggered by the specific efforts made by Niki and others to prevent her vomiting. The counselor wondered, How was Niki's vomiting being triggered by the well-meant efforts of the lunchroom worker to help her eat? How was Niki responding to her vomiting problem? Was there a link between how Niki's aunt and the school staff were responding to Niki's eating and the occurrence of the vomiting problem at school and at home? Could a different way of responding to the child's eating and vomiting be found that would eliminate the vomiting problem? This way of thinking and working is based on three assumptions that differ markedly from those supporting more familiar child or family counseling interventions.

First, persistent psychological problems (those that simple corrective actions do not resolve) are viewed as resulting when an everyday difficulty involving the student's adaptation to some life change is mishandled, the difficulty begins to be seen as a problem, and efforts made to solve the problem intensify it. Then a vicious circle is created in which the very behavior individuals use in attempting to resolve the difficulty actually makes it worse.

Second, these behavior patterns around a problem continue to be maintained because people believe that they are what should be done to resolve the problem. For example, a common solution used in responding to a child like Niki who upsets herself with fears of vomiting is to be comforting, telling the child to relax, and stop trying so hard not to vomit. However, sometimes (as in Niki's case) the more an effort is made to console the child and get her to relax, the more the youngster thinks, "They don't understand me and what I am going through." Thus, the action meant to alleviate the problem behavior can actually aggravate it. Such solutions may continue to be used even when they are not working because they are supported by commonsense wisdom.

Third, because the behaviors applied to alleviate the problem are assumed to be what maintain it, they are targeted for change. Acting on this third assumption, the practitioner would examine the symptomatic behavior and accompanying reactions and counter-reactions of everyone involved in the problem and determine whether actions in response to the student's problem behavior are inadvertently maintaining it. After gathering specific information about the student's problem and how it was being addressed, and learning what was not working, the practitioner would decide if a brief strategic intervention were warranted. If it were, the practitioner would then consider alternative ways of responding to the problem that would interrupt the original solution behaviors and substitute new ways of responding. To do this, the practitioner would provide an explanation to the persons involved that redefined the problem as well as the original motives and beliefs of the persons involved, thereby making new ways of responding more attractive. In addition, the practitioner would prescribe specific actions to implement this new plan.

These three assumptions—that the behaviors applied to solve a persistent problem often keep it going, that these solution behaviors are maintained because of beliefs that they are the most appropriate ones, and that inappropriate solution behaviors can be interrupted most quickly by reframing the problem and prescribing actions opposite to those originally applied—represent a radical departure from most accepted ways of helping students change their behavior. Because this way of thinking and working is different from what we are used to, let us examine how it is illustrated by the counselor who worked with Niki.

If you recall, in talking with Niki after the lunchroom aide departed, the counselor had learned that Niki became ill when the girls with whom she sat at lunch began to talk about their food. When she thought of the food, she would get a stomachache and throw up. Niki seemed very upset by these vomiting incidents and talked about being embarrassed by having had her friends see her vomiting. She also had said that it bothered her when the lunchroom helpers would coax her to eat her lunch. When asked to describe other times when she felt ill, Niki had identified two situations: in the classroom when she was nervous, and in her bed almost every night. In describing her nighttime vomiting, Niki had stated that her mother, a single parent, had taken an evening job two weeks earlier. Niki was left in the care of her aunt after school until bedtime. Her aunt was responsible for feeding both her and her cousins their dinner. Niki was unhappy because her aunt piled the food on her plate and forced her to sit at the dinner table until she had eaten it all. When Niki went to bed, she would feel sick and vomit. Her mother, upon returning home from work, would then change her bedsheets and care for her.

Using the brief strategic intervention approach, the counselor decided on four steps: to identify key elements in the interaction around the problem that inadvertently maintained the problem behavior; to formulate a solution shift that would interrupt the original solution efforts and substitute a new way of responding; to develop specific actions through which to implement this new way of responding and a rationale that would justify to the child and adults at school their relinquishing of old ways of responding to the problem; and to monitor the change effort.

As the counselor analyzed the information she had gotten from Niki and Mrs. Folsom, the lunchroom worker, she developed the following hypotheses about Niki's problem. First, Mrs. Folsom's comments—that she did not know what to make of Niki's vomiting, that Niki never ate all the food on her tray even when the staff told her she needed to eat a good lunch, and that the staff had tried to be understanding but that Niki had to stop her vomiting—suggested that the lunchroom staff might have attempted to resolve Niki's problem by pressuring her to eat. It appeared that not only had their well-meant efforts not worked, but they may have triggered Niki into doing even less of what they wanted by vomiting up the lunch they insisted she eat.

Niki's report of the lunchroom worker's efforts to make her "quit dawdling" and eat indicated she perceived she was being forced to eat when she did not want to. Her account of her aunt's efforts to make her eat revealed a similar perception. The basic thrust of the various efforts of adults in Niki's life—to make her eat or not vomit—were all variations on the theme of demanding that Niki comply. As Niki talked in her quiet, unassuming manner, it became clear why vomiting rather than openly defying these adults was the response triggered. Vomiting was a response that was perceived as involuntary, that is, outside of the child's control. It allowed Niki to obey these significant adults, yet not comply with their demands. A vicious circle had thus evolved in which the adults' well-meant efforts to get Niki to eat were met by her eating less (by vomiting) and by that act asserting that she could not rather than would not eat.

Because knowing what to avoid is the first step in deciding how to respond differently, the counselor realized it would be important to avoid giving Niki the message that she must comply with the expectation that she eat. It would also be important not to give the adults involved the message that they needed to be stronger in their efforts to get Niki to eat. But what was to work in place of these current responses?

Formulating a different way of defining Niki's vomiting and responding to it was the next step. It might appear that all that was required was for the adults involved not to pressure Niki to eat. However, this response would probably leave the vomiting behavior unchanged for several reasons. Because Niki would continue to believe that the adults in her life desired that she eat even though they said nothing about it, Niki would interpret a neutral stance to mean the adults involved were merely biding their time and had not really changed their position. To avoid giving this message, the counselor knew she would need to create a new and different frame in which to place any message for changed behavior. Knowing it would have to be a different frame from the pro-eating stance of the school and aunt, the counselor chose to side with Niki's anti-eating stance by telling her that she, Niki, was the only person who knew when she was hungry and how much food she needed. The counselor also identified specific action steps that were opposite to the ones currently being used in responding to the vomiting.

Why was this done? Because the type of solution applied to a problem is assumed to be what keeps the problem going, it is crucial to effect a maximum change in the current solution behaviors. By directing a person to reverse her current solution behavior in response to a problem—shifting it 180 degrees—a change is triggered in the problem behavior with which the solution behavior is entwined.

To implement this solution shift, the counselor had to specify concrete steps that would cause Niki and the school staff to act differently in response to the problem behavior. To do this, the counselor identified specific changes in the transactions around the problem behavior that could easily be incorporated into the school regimen. Next, a special rationale was developed to make these actions more attractive and to ensure their occurrence. The following dialogue illustrates how the counselor formulated these directives and introduced them by means of a rationale that made them more attractive to Niki.

Counselor: Niki, lots of people are trying to help you be healthy by telling you to eat all your food. They don't understand, though, that you know exactly when to eat and when to stop eating.

Niki: (Says nothing, but looks surprised as a smile breaks across her face.)

Counselor: So, Niki, I have a secret plan that will help you stop feeling sick and throwing up here at school.

Niki: It's a secret? What is it?

Counselor: We need to make some changes for a while. We will make these changes both in the lunchroom and in your classroom. You will be doing some things differently, taking charge of your sick feelings and taking care of yourself. Other people might forget and try to help too much, so it will be important to have a secret plan where you are taking care of yourself very well.

Niki: What is this plan?

Counselor: First, we will change lunchtime. I want you to eat lunch each day in the fresh air at the picnic tables outside. And because people are so used to trying to help you eat more than you want, I want you to eat by yourself. You are the expert who knows just what you need to eat and how much, so listen to your stomach and stop when it is full. It's OK to leave some food on your tray here at school.

Niki: What if I still need to throw up?

Counselor: That's what is so nice about the picnic tables. You can just throw up onto the sand and cover any mess yourself. Nobody will be angry with you because you will be taking care of yourself. I will be coming by for a few minutes every day to say "Hi" and to see how well you are doing. Do you think that you can be part of this secret plan?

Niki: Sure—except when it rains.

Counselor: Good thinking, Niki. We need a rain plan. How about if you come into my office when it rains at lunchtime? I will let you be alone so that you can practice deciding for yourself whether you are finished eating or not.

Niki: What about in the classroom?

Counselor: I will talk with your teacher, and she will be happy to change some things. For the next two weeks, any time you are feeling sick, I want you to quietly go to the door, open it, and step outside into the fresh air. I want you to take as many good, deep breaths of air as you need in order to feel better and return to your classroom. At first, you may need to throw up, but that's OK. Your teacher will know that you are taking care of yourself, and she will be glad when you return to the room. She will give you a secret wink like this. What do you think?

Niki: Will the other kids know about it?

Counselor: No, this secret will be just between you and your teacher.

Niki: I think I like that. I'll try it.

Counselor: You will like the plan more and more because each day you will feel better at school. You will be proud of the way you are taking care of yourself.

      After the counselor had met with Niki, she conferred with Niki's teacher and Mrs. Folsom, the lunchroom aide. To justify asking them to relinquish their old ways of responding to Niki's problem, the counselor employed a special explanation here as well. Because the counselor had noted that both women viewed Niki's problem benevolently (that is, Niki was upset, not bad, in continuing to vomit), she provided a benevolent rationale to justify her lunch plan for Niki. She did this by commenting that she had observed Niki to be an unusually sensitive child who was quite immature in learning to assume responsibility for herself and make her own decisions. To help Niki learn to be more responsible for herself, she and Niki had devised a plan for Niki to be in an independent eating situation. To maximize Niki's learning, it would be important that the lunchroom staff merely give Niki her lunch and provide no further direction to the child. The counselor indicated that she would take full responsibility for Niki at lunch for the time being. Then, after dismissing the lunchroom aide from this meeting, the counselor explained how the secret signal of winking would be used by Niki when she needed to leave the classroom, as a way to get her to take care of herself rather than solicit such caregiving from the teacher. The teacher agreed to meet with Niki for a few moments and secretly review how they would use the signal.

      To monitor Niki's progress, the counselor stopped by to see her every day when she was at the picnic table and chat with her about the fresh air, her successes in school, or a new joke the counselor had heard. When Niki referred to how much food she had eaten, the counselor restated that she, Niki, knew how much food she needed and when to stop eating. Each day the counselor noticed that Niki made fewer references to her health and ate a more balanced meal. Her teacher noted classroom improvement the second day the plan was in effect. During the third week, Niki said that she would like to return to eating with her friends. She said that she never felt ill anymore. For the next week she ate every other day in the lunchroom. The week after that she returned to the lunchroom table full time.

A visit one afternoon by the counselor to Niki's home occurred three weeks into the implementation of the plan. This visit allowed her to share with Niki's mother the success Niki had had at school. The counselor told the mother about the school vomiting problem and how Niki had resolved it. The mother said that Niki was still having the vomiting problem at home and seemed intrigued with the plan that had worked for her daughter at school. The mother discussed how she might modify it for home use. This modification included Niki being in control of her food intake, cleaning up after herself when she vomited, and receiving attention from her mother that did not center around anything to do with eating. Two weeks later the mother called to report that Niki had not vomited at home at all during the past weeks and that Niki seemed as happy with herself at home as she was at school.

The disappearance of Niki's problem vomiting in such a short time using brief strategic methods is not unusual. Often student problems can be eliminated merely by having the problematic behavior responded to differently. But how is this approach different from other child-focused intervention approaches such as behavior therapy or strategic family therapy? Why is it considered brief and strategic? Let us compare the theory and practice of brief strategic intervention with those of behavior therapy and strategic family therapy—two child-focused treatment approaches familiar to many school helping professionals. How do these three approaches differ in terms of the focus of treatment, the process of change, and the role of the practitioner in the change process?

These three approaches differ markedly in terms of what is considered the appropriate focus of treatment (see Table 1). For example, when a student demonstrates problem behavior at school and direct efforts to change that behavior are unsuccessful, behaviorally oriented practitioners consider

**Table 1. Differences Among Behavioral Therapy,
Brief Strategic Intervention, and Strategic Family Therapy.**

Brief Strategic Intervention	Behavioral Therapy	Strategic Family Therapy
Nature of Dysfunction		
Wrong solutions attempted in response to life's difficulties.	Improper individual conditioning.	Incongruent family hierarchy (for example, cross-generational coalition).
Nature of the Change Process		
Alter solution behavior.	Alter conditioning regimen.	Alter hierarchical arrangement.
Focus		
1. Process of interaction around the problem behavior.	1. Pattern of learning deficits.	1. Structure of family relationships.
2. Search for solution behavior in sequential behavior around the problem.	2. Search for reinforcement patterns in past and present.	2. Infer organizational hierarchy from current interactional sequence.
3. Present focus.	3. Focused on history of past learnings.	3. Present focus.
Methods of Change		
1. Directive.	1. Directive.	1. Directive.
2. Goals set, responsible for outcome.	2. Goals set, responsible for outcome.	2. Goals set, responsible for outcome.
3. Reframe to build motivation.	3. Motivation assumed.	3. Reframe to build motivation.
4. Uses both direct and indirect change methods.	4. Uses direct change methods.	4. Uses both direct and indirect change methods.
Change Agent Style		
Uses indirect, nonauthoritarian style.	Uses direct, expert style.	Uses both direct, expert and indirect, nonauthoritarian

the problem to be caused by some inner program to which the student is responding. Let us say, for instance, that John, a fourth grader, bullies his classmates despite repeated attempts to get him to stop. This problem is believed to be caused by some learning deficit in John, such as a lack of appropriate peer socializing skills. Given this individual view, methods of treating John's problem usually involve working with John either individually or through John's teacher or parents to modify these internal processes through systematic reinforcement. The practitioner either reinforces the way the student responds to him or requires the parents or teacher to follow a reinforcement schedule with the student. The focus is on bringing about change within the student (Keller, 1981).

In contrast, the brief strategic approach takes a distinctly different view of what is to be the focus of treatment. Persistent problematic behavior in students is perceived to result not from past faulty learning, but from current interactions between people. As Fisch and his associates state, "All behavior, both normal and problematic (and whatever its relations to the past or to individual personality factors) is continually being shaped and maintained (or changed) primarily by *ongoing* reinforcements in the particular behaving individual's systems of social interaction" (Fisch, Weakland, and Segal, 1982, p. 12) (italics mine). Instead of being seen as an intrinsic characteristic of the problem-bearer, problems are seen as occurring because of the mishandling of normal and predictable life difficulties. "Problems emerge when wrong attempts are made to alleviate a real or imagined difficulty and persist only because people continue to apply the same inappropriate methods to handle the difficulty which originally aggravated it" (Weakland, Fisch, Watzlawick, and Bodin, 1974, p. 149). Thus, from the brief strategic viewpoint, the real problem or focus of treatment is the cycle of interaction around the problem behavior engaged in by the problem-bearer and those involved with him (Watzlawick, Weakland, and Fisch, 1974).

Not only is this focus on changing the pattern of solution behaviors different from the focus of behavior therapy, it is also different from the focus of traditional family therapy. Most family therapists consider the underlying structure of family relationships the appropriate focus of the change effort (Haley, 1976; Madanes, 1981; Minuchin, 1974). Symptomatic behavior in a child is seen as indicative of a dysfunctional family organization in which the hierarchical arrangement of the family is confused. Thus, therapeutic efforts are focused on modifying the organizational structure of the family unit.

While not denying that past experience or current relationship structures can be a cause of a student's attitudes, behaviors, and needs, brief strategic practitioners believe that giving attention to such internal or structural variables only lengthens the treatment process. Also, it contributes to a less optimistic attitude about changing current attitudes and behaviors. As Segal (1982, p. 277) states, "Focusing on present interaction with the notion that people are simply 'keeping their wheels spinning' increases both the practitioner's optimism and the possibilities for intervening." Thus, rather than search for information that will allow the change agent to alter underlying intrapsychic structures or family relationship patterns, the counselor targets for change only the symptomatic behavior and its accompanying vicious circles of reaction and counter-reaction.

These differences regarding what is to be focused upon affect who is involved in the change process. Unlike behavioral or family systems approaches, which have predetermined assumptions about who is involved in the problem (and thus who must be involved in the change process), brief strategic intervention allows the composition of the group targeted for change to be variable. Rather than operating from a preconceived notion of who to involve, the practitioner examines how the student demonstrating the problem interacts with school personnel, peers, and people at home. If it appears that only the problem-bearer is responsible for maintaining her problematic behavior, then only that person is worked with. (A situation in which a student has some type of performance anxiety, but other people are not involved in helping her resolve this difficulty, would be a typical instance of a one-person focus.) In contrast, if two people are involved in a problem behavior (for example, if one student complains about another being insensitive to her, or if a teacher complains about a student's anxiety over a particular performance), then a two-person focus of intervention may be more appropriate. Finally, those situations in which more than two people are worked with often involve one person reporting a problem in relation to two or more other people. For example, a teacher may complain of her inability to quiet two students in her class who constantly bicker with one another. If the teacher is interested in changing the situation, all three parties may be involved in the change effort. Consequently, in brief strategic intervention as contrasted with strategic family therapy or behavior therapy, the number of persons who make up the intervention unit depends exclusively on who is involved in maintaining the problem behavior. Furthermore, because it is assumed that a variety of different people (for example, family, teachers, counselors, and other students) may be involved in a student's problem, interventions may be aimed at changing the problem-maintaining responses of school staff and students instead of, or as well as, family members. Such school-focused interventions may be used either because the school's response is the primary one maintaining the student's problematic behavior, or because the student's behavior is being responded to similarly at school and at home and the school staff's efforts are more available for immediate change.

Although each of these approaches share in common a focus on resolving the presenting problem, deliberately planning interventions to fit the particular problem, and having the practitioner assume an active role in designing and directing the change effort, ideas as to how change in the problem behavior is to come about differ considerably. Typically, behavior therapists assume that change can be brought about in a straightforward fashion through processes of conditioning and deconditioning. Once a problematic behavior and a pattern of reinforcement are identified, institution of a more appropriate pattern of reinforcement is expected to proceed straightforwardly, with people showing little or no resistance to the therapist's directives. Enlightenment is all that is necessary for change to proceed. But what if a child's teacher and parents feel the prescribed conditioning is not what she needs?

In contrast, great care is given in both strategic family therapy and brief strategic intervention to anticipating how people may respond to a therapist's directives and to planning strategies that aim to motivate them to try new ways of behaving. The innovative work of Milton Erickson has prompted efforts to observe the idiosyncratic characteristics and motivation of each person involved in the intervention, and to use these characteristics as levers for change. This is frequently done by making all behavioral instructions appear indirect, implicit, or apparently insignificant, rather than by issuing authoritative directions. The therapist uses participant beliefs about the problem or problem person to develop explanations that reframe the meaning associated with the actions suggested. These explanations are specifically designed to suit the problem situation and the people involved. Typically, the therapist gathers information from each person as to why she believes the problem exists and how she thinks it can and cannot be resolved. Then the therapist uses this information to design a change message to motivate each person involved to try something different.

This procedure is a hallmark of the strategic approach to intervention. Brief strategic practitioners assume that the reason people often persist in an approach to solving a problem long after it has proved unsuccessful is that they feel theirs is the only right way to respond to the problem. For this reason, and because discarding old ways and trying new ones can require great effort, practitioners use indirect as well as direct tactics to bring about change. Direct tactics may focus on prescribing specific tasks that certain people are to follow through on between sessions. Indirect tactics involve opposition and rely on the individual's defiance of the therapist. Such tactics may be used to trigger in either the problem-bearer or some other involved person a less problematic response to the problem behavior. To do this, the practitioner considers which responses are most central to maintenance of the problem, thinks in transactional terms about how to change what people say and do in trying to resolve a problem, and provides specific directions to participants concerning when and how to act differently. This process is illustrated in the case of Niki: Merely telling her to stop worrying about vomiting would have done little to interrupt her efforts to control her vomiting. Instead, the counselor directed Niki to carry out a set of responses that could be performed in place of the original behaviors. These responses had to implement the goal of reversing the predictable sequence of interactions that supported the problem, as well as create a new situation that elicited a new set of responses.

Although all three approaches advocate deliberate intervention by the practitioner, they differ in how direct or indirect they are. By far the most direct approach is that of the behavior therapist, who will often give explicit instructions to different persons to start or stop certain actions or behaviors. This approach relies on individuals complying with the directives. Strategic family therapists assume a middle ground. They use direct strategies, which allow them to realign power differentials within the family, but they also use indirect strategies, which benefit the client regardless of whether she chooses to comply with or defy her instructions.

In the brief strategic approach, the practitioner's influence is consciously indirect. Although the practitioner may very well give direct assignments to perform new actions, the delivery of such assignments is consciously nonauthoritarian. Consider, for example, the way the counselor discussed the possibility of Niki eating outside. This was framed as if it were something completely up to Niki to decide. This is the hallmark of the brief strategic approach. Rather than go nose-to-nose to convince a client of the necessity of changing his ways, the practitioner adopts a nonauthoritarian position to increase collaboration, relying on tentatively made suggestions or questions rather than direct orders, or even on an appearance of ignorance and confusion. In addition, it is crucial in brief strategic intervention for the practitioner to convey an implied agreement with, and a subtle reframing of, the client's position. Thus, the way in which the practitioner gives suggestions or directives is always well considered.

In summary, brief strategic intervention is a distinctive new way of thinking and working to bring about change in students. Although it shares with behavior therapy an emphasis on changing concrete, observable behaviors, and with strategic family therapy an emphasis on using indirect tactics, it differs markedly from these two approaches in its definition of what is to be focused upon and altered. Because this approach is briefer than most strategic family therapy efforts, yet more adaptable to working with resistant persons and beliefs than behavior therapy, it represents a distinctive new alternative for resolving persistent problems students experience at school.

To use this approach effectively, school helping professionals must understand the distinctive premises about the development of problems and their resolution on which this approach is based. In addition they need to understand how these premises are translated into actual practice. In the next chapter, we describe these basic premises in more detail and illustrate how they affect one's intervention practices.

CHAPTER 2

Defining and Resolving Persistent School Problems

The brief strategic approach requires that one put on a different set of glasses to view students' problems and their resolution. To use this approach effectively, the school practitioner must understand the basic premises about the nature of problems and their resolution that characterize this approach. These premises influence the kinds of data the practitioner looks for, whom she chooses to involve in her intervention, what she actually says and does, and how she evaluates her efforts. In this chapter, I will describe these premises in more detail and then illustrate how they affect practice.

As mentioned earlier, the brief strategic view of what constitutes problems and useful help differs greatly from that proposed by many established child intervention theories. Basic to the brief strategic viewpoint is the belief that a person's behavior (whether normal or problematic) is maintained and structured by interaction with other people. This means that members of a student's family, people that he interacts with at school, or persons in his neighborhood may each have a hand in shaping the student's behavior. The student, in turn, shapes the behavior of these other individuals; as these people continue to interact over time, certain repetitive patterns develop around both normal and problematic behaviors.

Because brief strategic practitioners view problems as interactional, that is, not inherent to a particular person, they consistently consider all of the actions of participants in the student's key social systems. This view of the problem-bearer as a part of a larger interactional whole rather than as a whole unto herself is a characteristic feature of systemic thinkers. It contrasts sharply with the traditional nonsystemic views prevalent in psychology and education, which treat the individual as a whole consisting of parts.

What are the consequences of adopting an interactional point of view? One consequence is that problem behavior is explained not in terms of personality structure but in terms of efforts by the problem-bearer and those with whom she interacts to solve the problem. Given this premise, brief strategic practitioners always study the individual's problem behavior within the context in which it is occurring and focus their attention on discerning the connections and relationships between the occurrence of the problem behavior and the behavior of other persons in regular interaction with the problem-bearer.

A second consequence is that all persons involved with the problem person on a regular basis, both at home and at school, are considered members of the "problem-determined" interactional system (Anderson, Goolishan, and Windermand, 1987). Persons at school as well as at home often have a hand in defining the student's school problem and attempting to resolve it. Thus, interventions may be aimed at changing the solution efforts of school staff as well as of a student's family.

Let us see how such an interactional view is actually applied in explaining student problem behavior. In the following dialogue, a single-parent mother is contacted by phone by the school counselor concerning her fifteen-year-old son's refusal to attend school. Observe how the mother describes the issue: How does she view her son's refusal to attend school? Does she act concerned, or does she diminish its importance? How does she appear to view her son? Is he seen as contrary or confused and troubled? What does she say to her son about this issue? What exactly does she do or not do? In turn, how does her son respond to her efforts? Does he view her as ineffectual or controlling? Does he view the school situation as hopeless? Unimportant? What in turn, is the impact of his actions on his mother?

Counselor: Mrs. Thompson, you seem pretty concerned about Sam's not attending school.

Mother: Yes, I am. I know he needs to go to school, but I just can't seem to get him to go.

Counselor: You've tried some different things to get him to go?

Mother: Oh, yes. You don't know how many times I've tried to tell him he needs to go to school, but nothing seems to work.

Counselor: To help me get a little bit better idea of what seems to be happening with Sam, I wonder if you would describe a specific time when you were dealing with him about this issue.

Mother: Well, yesterday we were talking about this. I wanted him to go to school and get back on track. He's been out for too long now. I'm sure he's way behind in his work.

Counselor: Could you tell me what you said to him? Just to help me get a little clearer picture of how he responds to your efforts?

Mother: Well, yesterday when he and I were eating lunch together at home, I said, "Sam, you know that you need to go to school."

Counselor: And what did he do?

Mother: He said he just couldn't stand it there, that it was like being in a prison.

Counselor: And then?

Mother: Well, I know that every school has things about it you can't like. So I told him that. But I don't think he's really given it a chance.

Counselor: So did you say that?

Mother: Yes, I asked him if he had really given it a chance, and he said that he had, but he just couldn't take it anymore.

Counselor: And then?

Mother: Well, I started to get really frustrated again because this is where it always goes when I try and get him to go back to school. So I found myself getting angry and starting to push him. I told him that he had to do something with his life, and I asked him what he was going to do.

Counselor: And how did he respond?

Mother: He just said his typical thing: "I will, I will. Just don't rush me." Well, that just made me madder. So I said, "Son, you've been out of school doing nothing for two months now." He seemed to get a little sad with that, like I'd hurt him or hit a nerve or something, because he said, "I know. I'm going to find out what I want to do pretty soon." I just couldn't stop then though, so I said, "But when? Your life and your opportunities are just slipping by!"

Counselor: Then what happened?

Mother: Well, I guess I made him mad with that because he said, "Oh, Mom, don't get dramatic. I'll do it. Don't worry." I knew I'd pushed him far enough, so I just dropped it. Nothing got settled, but I could see that I was just turning him off.

Counselor: Is this the way it seems to usually go? You trying to help him see that he needs to be doing something to get on with his life, and him backing off from your help?

Mother: Yes, I really have tried to help him get going, but nothing seems to work.

A pattern of behaviors that is both vicious and circular is demonstrated in these interactions between mother and son. The mother does not directly request that her son attend school; instead, she attempts to get him interested in attending school by explaining why he should attend and repeatedly asking him what he wants to do. She seems to operate on the assumption that he must want to go to school and thus she cannot (and does not) directly demand that he go. Consequently, she indirectly requests that he attend school through the attention she gives to this topic in her conversation. The son, in turn, does not directly reject this indirect request from his mother; instead he constantly provides evidence that school is not what he wants to do or feels he can endure. This response, in turn, affirms his mother's belief that he would attend school if he could, but somehow he cannot.

The view proposed here is that the problem behavior (that is, the actual refusal to attend school) and the efforts made by both mother and son to get rid of the problem are intertwined; they trigger each other's occurrence. Thus, a circular or cybernetic rather than linear concept of causation is implied here (Maruyama, 1963; Wender, 1968). In this cybernetic paradigm, part and whole are assumed to be linked by a closed informational loop or feedback circuit. The part performs some action that has an impact on the whole; the whole then reacts back on the part, which has a subsequent action that affects the whole; and so on. In using this cybernetic paradigm, brief strategic theorists ask us to change the way we think about causality. Rather than consider behavior as linearly caused (that is, event A causes or leads to event B, but B does not cause A), brief strategic thinking considers it as a loop (that is, A leads to B *and* B leads to A). As Keeney and Ross (1985, p. 88) so aptly state, "In the MRI [brief strategic] approach, the problem and efforts to solve it are seen as recursively entwined: The problem arises out of efforts to solve it, while attempted solutions arise from experiencing the problem." It is this cycle of interaction that is the target of the brief strategic practitioner's intervention efforts.

But how do such cycles originate? And why do they become problematic? Brief strategic theorists contend that problems develop when normal life difficulties are mishandled. Such difficulties include both predictable developmental transitions (for example, a child starting to attend school, the birth of a new baby sister or brother, or the death of a family member) and nondevelopmental crises (for example, a car accident, a natural disaster, or a divorce in the family). When these normal life difficulties are mishandled and an unsuccessful solution is persisted in, problems develop.

This vicious circle might be viewed as similar to what happens when a house gets overly warm inside and a person flings open a window to cool it down. If the house's heating thermostat is on, the cool air from the open window will trigger the heater to turn on and attempt to heat the house even more. If someone subsequently opens another window to dissipate the heat, the heater will be triggered to come on and attempt to make the house even warmer. Thus, opening the window—while a perfectly effective solution in and of itself—is the wrong solution for this particular set of conditions. The more the solution of opening a window is applied, the warmer the house stays. Therefore, the solution actually triggers the problem to get worse.

For example, in the situation described above involving Sam and his mother, Sam's dislike of school is certainly a common difficulty many teenagers experience and try to solve by refusing to attend school. What makes this situation problematic? The view proposed here is that Sam's mother's effort to resolve his problem by trying to accommodate his preferences while also indirectly commanding that he attend school actually triggers more refusal behavior in Sam and in all likelihood will lead him to be even more out of step with his peers.

Although it is easy to accept that some people do not handle the normal difficulties of life well, it is harder to believe that they will continue to handle their difficulties the same way even when their solutions are obviously not working. One may be tempted to theorize that there must be some underlying defect either in the problem person's personality (for example, poor self-esteem, low motivation, poor ego strength) or in her family organization (for example, rigid role structure or interpersonal advantage) which makes her continue to persist blindly in her errors despite evidence of their failure.

How can this continued mishandling of life difficulties be explained if not as the result of some fundamental defect in the family organization or the individuals involved? How is it that people persist in ineffective ways of solving a problem even when they are obviously not working? For example, why does Sam's mother continue to avoid insisting that her youngster attend school, although knowing full well that her current efforts at accommodating to his preferences are not working? And why does Sam continue to avoid attending school despite the fact that his current efforts do not result in his mother giving him any peace?

The brief strategic view is that people persist in actions that maintain problems inadvertently and often with the best of intentions for two reasons. First, they may not realize that what they are doing is actually contributing to keeping the problem going. Second, even when they are aware of this, they often feel that it is still the only right way they can respond. For example, Sam's mother may very well believe that what little interest her son demonstrates in attending school is a direct result of her efforts to be understanding and supportive. This persistence in the face of contrary evidence is, according to brief strategic theorists (Fisch, Weakland, and Segal, 1982; Watzlawick, Weakland, and Fisch, 1974), more a matter of logical error than anything else. That is, people often go about attempting to deal with a problem in a manner consistent with their view of reality and what they believe to be the right way to behave. Thus, people adhere to a certain course of action even when it is not helping because they believe it should work. The attempted solution is maintained because it is considered the only logical, necessary, or appropriate thing to do. For example, Sam's mother (like many people) believes that if you force someone to do something he will not like doing it. In cases like this, when an approach is heavily supported by cultural tradition and so-called common sense, it will continue to be followed despite not working.

Furthermore, when such an approach fails, the problem-bearer and the other people involved usually interpret the failure as an indication of the severity of the problem rather than the inappropriateness of the solution. Then even more of the same solution is applied, and the problem becomes a self-perpetuating system of interaction. As Segal (1982, p. 280) vividly writes, "The problem-bearer is like a man caught in quicksand. The more he struggles, the more he sinks; the more he sinks, the more he struggles." In their book *The Tactics of Change,* Fisch and his associates explain this circumstance in the following way: "Poor solutions are followed very carefully, and this is quite expectable for people who are understandably anxious in the midst of difficulties. Beliefs in such solutions also make it hard to see that they are not serving as effective guides. Furthermore, it is easy to rationalize away the direct experience of continuing trouble by saying that it is only the present efforts which keep things from being even worse" (Fisch, Weakland, and Segal, 1982, p. 18).

Elsewhere in *The Tactics of Change,* the problem is defined in terms of four features: "First, it must be an expressed concern about some behavior (for example, actions, thoughts, or feelings) which a person has about himself or another with whom he/she is significantly involved. Second, this behavior must be defined either as deviant (that is, unusual or inappropriate) and/or distressing (that is, immediately or potentially harmful) either by the person demonstrating the problem behavior or by others with whom that person is involved. Third, efforts made to alter this behavior must have been unsuccessful. Fourth, due to this lack of success in changing the problem behavior, outside help is sought either by the problem person or others with whom that person is involved" (p. 11).

Consequently, in the case of the youngster refusing to attend school, how the behavior is described as a problem, how people report having attempted to resolve the problem, who is now seeking help for the problem, and what is expected in the way of help are each key elements in defining the problem.

In this approach, the targets of the practitioner's efforts are the solutions people apply to problems despite their lack of success. To alter such solution efforts, the practitioner must change the client's current solution frame. But why is this necessary? This question is best answered through an analogy. In *Change,* Watzlawick, Weakland, and Fisch (1974) present the so-called nine-dot problem (see Figure 1). Try it now, before reading further. Connect the nine dots in Figure 1 without lifting your pencil from the paper, using four straight lines.

Now look at the actual solution (see Figure 2, p. 40). The solution pictured in Figure 2 is not one most people manage to come up with by themselves. According to Watzlawick and his associates, this is because almost everyone who tries to solve this problem introduces assumptions as to how the problem is to be solved that make the solution of the task impossible. These assumptions are that the dots compose a square and that the solution must therefore be found within that square. Interestingly, these are self-imposed assumptions that were not stated in the instructions. However, given these assumptions, it does not matter what combination of four lines is tried; there will always be at least one unconnected dot left over. Why? Because one's failure does not lie in the impossibility of the task, but in the set of assumptions as to how it should be solved—one's solution frame. However, if one frees oneself from the solution frame and tries something outside it, one can arrive at the appropriate solution—as Figure 2 shows.

Figure 1. The Nine-Dot Problem.

The nine dots are to be connected without lifting the pencil from the paper and by using four distinct straight lines.

Source: Watzlawick, Weakland, and Fisch, 1974.

This nine-dot problem demonstrates a number of lessons. If you understand these, you will have grasped the major principle underlying brief strategic intervention. Let us discuss them one by one. First, as the nine-dot problem clearly demonstrates, all problems are defined within a particular frame or context. This frame may be explicit or implicit. For example, the nine-dot problem had an explicit frame which consisted of the pattern of nine dots and the set of instructions given in Figure 1. In addition, in many people's minds there was also an implicit frame—the belief that the nine dots formed a square that marked a boundary the four lines could not cross. Thus, as we can see here, no problem exists in a vacuum; it always has a solution frame as well.

Second, it is clear that a problem unsolvable in one frame may have a solution in a different frame. The nine-dot problem was unsolvable as long as it was assumed that the dots formed a square within which the solution was to be found. However, once this assumption was abandoned, the problem could be solved. Thus this analogy beautifully illustrates how the constraints of a particular frame may preclude solution of a particular problem.

Two other lessons found in the nine-dot analogy concern the process of changing a solution. First, you may have observed that your change in frames required input from outside your current frame. Often, the harder one tries to solve the problem from within the frame, the more one tends to get locked into the assumptions of the frame, and the more difficult—or indeed impossible—it becomes to break out. It often takes someone who is not locked into this solution frame to present a new way of solving a problem. Second, a change in frames often occurs suddenly, in an all-or-nothing fashion: One either sees it or one does not. This is a very different model of learning from the one commonly used in education. Typically, learning is seen as a gradual accumulation of habits over many trials and efforts to shape behaviors. But this way of learning is different. Once the problem is seen in a new frame that works (that is, solves the problem), it is almost impossible to revert back to the old frame.

Thus, the key task of the brief strategic practitioner is to examine the presenting complaint and decide whether it can be solved within that frame. If not, the practitioner needs to reframe the problem so that it can be solved. To do this, the practitioner must be able to free herself from the original frame given to the problem situation and give it a new meaning that fits the facts as well as or better than the old frame yet brings about a cognitive and emotional change that prevents a recurrence of the old solution behaviors. Let us see how this idea can be applied in a school setting.

A school counselor was contacted by phone by the mother of an eighth-grade student named Scott. According to Scott's mother, he seemed headed for D's in four out of six subjects for his first semester's work. His grades in the remaining two subjects, physical education and art, were C's. Scott's academic records revealed that he was well above average in intelligence, although he had achieved an unspectacular academic record in seventh grade (mostly C's, with one D and one B) despite his parents' constant efforts to get him to do well. His only passion in school and out was playing basketball. After receiving Scott's interim grade report, Scott's mother had had a conference with Scott's teachers. As a result of this conference, the parents had made several specific efforts to get Scott more involved in his schoolwork, setting up a routine of regular study sessions after school and instituting a system in which Scott was grounded for the weekend when any weekly test grade fell below a C. More recently, Scott's parents had punished him when his grades fell below a C by not allowing him to play basketball. Scott's mother reported that he had responded to all these efforts by performing even more poorly and acting nonchalant when his parents instituted the ultimate consequence of not allowing him to play basketball.

Hearing this information, the counselor realized that Scott and his parents were caught in a vicious circle. The more the parents pressured Scott to do better academically, the more he resisted their demands. Although the various efforts made by the parents to get their son to improve his academic performance were common ones parents employ, with Scott these tactics appeared to have exactly the opposite effect to the one intended. The more the parents demanded he perform, the less Scott did. In thinking about this situation, the counselor noted that the basic thrust of all of the parents' efforts was to demand that their son comply with their wishes that he do better in school. They assumed that they knew what was best for him, that they were right, and that he should comply with their demands. However, rather than resulting in compliance, these efforts seemed to trigger in Scott the urge to gain the upper hand by ignoring their requests.

Knowing what to avoid is the first step in deciding how to respond differently to a problem situation. In Scott's case, the counselor realized that it would be important to avoid giving the parents the message to push Scott harder to comply with their demands. But what would work in place of this kind of response? How could a different way of responding to the problem situation be found—one that would not trigger more of the problem behavior?

Although the idea of having those involved do something different in response to a problem behavior sounds simple enough, it is often very difficult for them to think of, much less try out, a different way of responding to the problem. More often than not people can think of only two options—either doing more of the same or not responding. For example, in discussing with Scott's parents what they had tried, they only came up with two alternatives—continuing to demand that their son do better academically or not saying anything (but inwardly worrying). When asked to think of other ways of dealing with this problem, Scott's parents thought only of variations on these two themes of coercing Scott into improving his grades or trying to ignore the matter. They assumed that these were the only right solutions possible.

The idea that there might be any number of other possible courses of action was very difficult for Scott's parents to see. One might guess that they thought this way because the solution of a parent demanding compliance from a child in this type of situation is suggested by our culture, because no other alternative made sense to them, because they felt compelled to do something, and because ignoring the situation did not resolve it. But how might Scott's parents respond so that Scott was not provoked to do even less of what they wanted? To be able to think of a less problem-provoking response for Scott's parents, the counselor first needed to get outside the parents' current solution frame of either coercing or ignoring Scott. As in the nine-dot problem, this frame actually prevented solution of the problem.

But how does one develop a new solution frame for a client? One way is to mentally try reversing the thrust of the client's attempted solution. In Scott's case, the counselor decided to direct Scott's parents to reverse their current thrust by agreeing with Scott's anti-achievement stance. The parents were to shift from taking a one-up position (that is, demanding to be obeyed) to taking a one-down position (that is, allowing Scott to have authority). Such a reversal was necessary because if they merely stopped pressuring their son to perform better academically, Scott would probably interpret this to mean that they were merely biding their time. Such a perception would have resulted in no change in Scott's current stance about academics and eventually, when his parents became discouraged, would have drawn them back into using their old solution of pressuring him to do better.

This type of intervention is effective because it is based on the premise that since the solution applied to a problem is what actually keeps it going, to effect the most change in the problem behavior one needs to effect a maximum change in the current solution behavior. By directing a person to reverse her solution behavior, a shift in the opposing problem behavior can be elicited. This way of intervening to modify problem behavior is regularly illustrated in the therapeutic tactics of systemic therapists such as Bowen (1978), DeShazer (1982), Papp (1983), and Selvini-Palazolli and others (1978), as well as Watzlawick, Weakland, and Fisch (1974).

Why does this tactic work? Think of two canoeists trying to steer a straight course down a river. Each is paddling as hard as he can on an opposing side of the canoe in order to steer a straight course. The more vigorously one canoeist paddles, the more the canoe turns to that side, forcing the other canoeist to paddle more vigorously to compensate for being pulled off course by the other's attempt to steer a straight course. The canoe would actually be much easier to keep on course if not for the two canoeists' frantic efforts to keep it there. However, each canoeist thinks the only way he can keep on course is to paddle harder.

To change this crazy situation, Watzlawick, Weakland, and Fisch (1974) would suggest that at least one of the canoeists do something seemingly quite unreasonable, namely paddle less. This would immediately force the other to also paddle less—unless he wanted to end up going in circles. Eventually, they would find themselves comfortably paddling on a straight course.

However, the impact of paddling just a little less vigorously is not likely to be noticed as readily by one's canoe mate as a switch to paddling on his side of the canoe would be. Similarly, modifying the current solution behavior just a little is not likely to quickly trigger a marked counter-response. What is needed is to take a noticeably different position. Reversing one's response to a problem provides the clearest message of such a change.

In real life, however, most people have a great deal of difficulty trying a new solution that flies in the face of their current operating premises. Because people think their current way of handling the problem is the only safe and sane thing to do, they will strongly resist being told to stop doing what they are now doing and take an opposite stance. Consequently, for a reversal to be acted upon, a new frame must be developed that makes such a stance acceptable to the client. To do this, the counselor must carefully attend to how the persons involved perceive the problem, its cause, and its cure. What are their reasons for responding the way they do? Whose interests do they have in mind? What are viewed as the ultimate benefits of maintaining their positions? What pitfalls are to be avoided?

In Scott's case, his parents saw themselves as intelligent problem-solvers whose high academic expectations for their son were quite reasonable and necessary. They viewed it as important that they should be in an authoritative position with respect to Scott. To make their required shift to a one-down position more palatable, it was necessary to introduce the reversal as a tactic they could use to win the battle with Scott. Therefore, before suggesting the reversal, the counselor complimented both parents on being quite knowledgeable and sophisticated psychologically and thus able to grasp what she would be suggesting that they do. She then stated that while they really knew what was best for their son, it appeared that he was locked in a power struggle with them and that he was winning. Because they were older and more savvy psychologically than he, they could win the struggle. However, it would require that they use reverse psychology on him. Specific steps the parents could take in carrying out this reverse psychology tactic were then proposed. (This particular approach was inspired by Peggy Papp of the Ackerman Institute, New York, New York, who reported using a similar procedure in working with parents concerned about their child's academic failure.)

After providing the above-mentioned rationale and noting that the parents' response to it was positive, the counselor suggested the following course of action. Instead of constantly emphasizing how Scott should live up to his high potential, the parents were encouraged to find ways to give Scott the message that he restrain his potential and put the lid on his development. Although the parents were initially surprised and somewhat hesitant to follow this particular approach, they acknowledged that Scott was winning the war and that they needed to do something to get control back.

In discussing with the counselor how they could give Scott the message of restraint, the parents volunteered that one thing they were very concerned about was that Scott would fail eighth grade and not be able to move on into high school. The father then proposed that they could tell their son that they had been doing a lot of thinking about his situation and had come to the conclusion that it would not be so awful after all if he failed and had to repeat the eighth grade. Scott's mother agreed with this suggestion and, in thinking of a reason to give him, proposed that they would say they were not upset because they thought children were growing up too fast as it was nowadays.

This case illustrates how the school practitioner identifies specific ways in which the persons involved can modify what they say or do in relationship to a problem. The practitioner first thinks of what steps she could get the persons involved to take that would be the greatest departure from their previous stance. These steps should occur with enough frequency to have some impact on the usual problem/solution sequence.

Getting people to act in relevant new ways through the use of direct suggestion and monitoring these behavior changes are key features of this approach. In Scott's case, Scott's mother and father reported that they carried out the planned reverse psychology tactic to the letter. They reported saying to Scott that they had decided that the longer he remained a child the better, because that way he could stay close to the family, and if he had to attend summer school, at least they would know he was safe and not off playing basketball with some of his crazy friends.

The parents reported that Scott initially reacted to these statements with suspicion and disbelief. But the parents persisted in maintaining their antiachievement attitude. After four weeks they began to notice Scott improving his grades and suggested that he might be rushing things to be planning to move into ninth grade. After all, he could go to summer school and make up some of his failures. Scott heatedly reported that he was not going to make himself waste his whole summer vacation in school. A follow-up with Scott's teachers after eight weeks had elapsed revealed he had made a radical turnaround. He was consistently doing B work in all his classes.

This case illustrates the four key steps involved in altering an unworkable solution: identifying the problem/solution cycle and nature of the current solution thrust, formulating an alternative way of framing the problem and responding to it that shifts the current solution efforts, prescribing specific actions to implement this solution shift and a rationale to motivate those involved to try the new way of responding, and sustaining and monitoring the new behaviors. To highlight these steps, we will discuss another case in which the practitioner formulated an alternative way of framing a student's problem behavior and responding to it and developed a specific rationale and action steps implementing this new way of responding.

Often student problems are maintained by a special triangular context in which one person is in conflict with another person while a third person tries to keep the two opponents from fighting. In this situation, almost any comment by either of the opponents, and especially a comment expressing disagreement, can rapidly flare up into a stormy battle that only ends for a short while. This conflict situation is often unknowingly maintained by the efforts of the person playing the role of peacekeeper. Upset by the stress of the fighting and wanting to see a better relationship between the two antagonists, this peacekeeper usually tries to calm the waters by reasoning with one or both parties. Instead of having a calming effect, however, this reasoning has an inflammatory one. This pattern can be demonstrated in the interaction of a student, a school professional (for example, a teacher) and a second school professional (for example, a school counselor); a student and her parents; a student, a parent, and a school professional; or two children and an adult (for example, two students and a teacher, or two siblings and a parent). This pattern is illustrated in the following case involving a student and his parents.

Kevin, seventeen, was constantly embroiled with the school administration because of his devil-may-care attitude— hot rodding his car through the school parking lot, skipping school, and being disrespectful to teachers. In a school conference with Kevin and his parents, Kevin's father admitted that his son's behavior at home (lying, associating with undesirable friends, and being generally surly, irresponsible, and inconsiderate) was no better than that at school. Although both Kevin's mother and father talked of wanting fewer hassles with Kevin, better behavior at school, and better communication with him, Kevin's father seemed to believe that such changes were impossible. He cited a long list of Kevin's mishaps as evidence that the situation was hopeless. Kevin took exception to every charge his father made, and the pair quickly became embroiled in a nasty interchange. Kevin's mother endured this interchange only momentarily and then stepped in to reason with one or the other of them. The mother's reasoning consisted, in turn, of trying to convince her husband there was some hope for Kevin if he would recognize his son's special needs and be less harsh and critical, and explaining to Kevin that his father really loved him and asking Kevin to be more patient and watch what he said. To Kevin, this reasoning implied criticism of his role in the argument and a coalition between the two parents. To the father, being taken to task for the way he was handling Kevin indicated a coalition between his wife and Kevin.

Consequently, although the mother's peacekeeping efforts were well meant, they served to further polarize the relationship between Kevin and his father while convincing the mother that even more peacekeeping help was needed by the two. Thus a vicious circle was maintained: The more the father and son battled, the more the mother carried out her peacekeeping efforts, and the more she did that, the more her efforts triggered new conflicts between father and son.

Because the mother believed that it was only her efforts that kept her husband and son's conflicts from becoming even more hurtful, she was very invested in staying in the middle. To help the mother shift away from her position, the practitioner developed specific action directives and a rationale to motivate her.

The plan was to coach the mother to stay in the middle but to assume an unreasonable rather than a reasonable position. To implement this shift in behavior, a conference was held with just the mother. During this conference, the school psychologist attempted to shift the mother's viewpoint on the problem. The psychologist did this by sympathizing with the mother and acknowledging that she must be tired of being in the middle, but indicating that she would not be able to leave that position until her husband and son no longer needed her as an intermediary. But as long as they relied on her to be their go-between, it was not necessary for them to learn how to negotiate for themselves—after all, why bother, when she did such a good job? The psychologist spent a great deal of time belaboring the advantages of their position and the relative discomfort of hers. He then mentioned—almost as an aside—that if only she would not be such a good negotiator, they might become aware of the load she carried. The mother's curiosity was piqued and she inquired what the psychologist meant by the comment. He explained that if she were to become unreasonable as a negotiator, her husband and son might feel it would be in their best interest to do their own negotiating. To implement this idea, it was suggested that the mother adopt an unreasonable position—agreeing with each person's point of view and suggesting that perhaps each had not gone far enough.

The mother agreed to carry out this plan and report back several days later. When she did, she indicated that she had tried to be unreasonable and was surprised by the result.

Figure 2. One Solution to the Nine-Dot Problem.

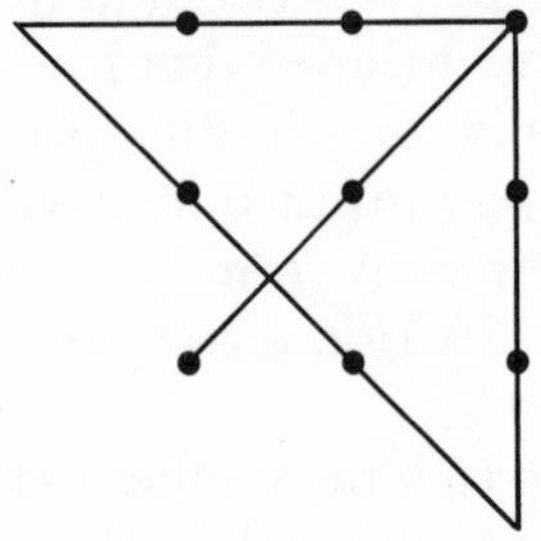

Source: Watzlawick, Weakland, and Fisch, 1974.

For example, on one occasion she had agreed with her husband's exasperation over an incident Kevin was embroiled in and suggested that the father was not being stern enough in dealing with Kevin. To her surprise, her husband disagreed with her. The subsequent week she reported a reduced number of arguments between her husband and son; however, she continued to "botch her job" (as she called it) of go-between. Over the next several weeks she noticed a significant decrease in arguments between them. In addition, Kevin became involved with some new friends who were more acceptable to his parents, and his teachers reported him less antagonistic with them and with other students.

In summary, the premises about problem formation and resolution determine the kinds of data the school practitioner looks for, who he involves in his intervention, and what he says and does. However, not only must the school practitioner have a clear view of the interactional patterns in which problematic student behaviors are embedded, he must also determine what would be the most strategic shift in the current solution efforts and take steps to instigate that change. In the remainder of this book, these basic steps are described in detail.

PART TWO

Brief Strategic Intervention in Practice

In the first two chapters you became acquainted with the basic premises on which brief strategic intervention is based and saw how these premises were translated into practice. In addition, the particular sequence of steps comprising this approach were illustrated. These steps are: gathering information about interaction around a student's problem to ascertain whether a brief strategic approach is warranted, identifying the problem/solution cycle, formulating a solution shift involving specific action directives and a rationale to motivate those involved to follow those directives, and monitoring and evaluating the change effort.

In Chapters Three through Eight, each of these steps is explained in more detail. Chapter Three focuses on how one goes about deciding when to use brief strategic tactics. Chapter Four addresses the general issue of the school practitioner's control over the intervention process and the common issues that arise early in shaping the amount of influence she can have. This topic is placed early in this section because often the practitioner's control over the intervention process can go awry either during the initial contact regarding a student or in early meetings concerning him. Chapter Five describes the kinds of information that are needed to resolve student problems briefly; it also considers methods for collecting this information. Chapter Six gives special emphasis to gathering information about those client beliefs central to maintenance (and thus to resolution) of a student's problem. This information is essential both in enhancing client compliance with one's intervention directives and in avoiding client resistance. Chapter Seven describes how these types of information are analyzed and used to formulate specific tactics to resolve a student's problem. Finally, Chapter Eight examines various techniques for monitoring and evaluating the intervention process.

CHAPTER 3

Deciding When to Use
Brief Strategic Intervention

It is only when student problems do not respond to simple, commonsense problem-solving methods such as providing advice or emotional support or making direct requests for changed behavior that people begin to view the student's problem as entrenched and consider using more intensive therapeutic approaches. Thus, brief strategic intervention, like other, longer-term treatment approaches, is actually a second stage of working to resolve student problems. But when should brief strategic methods be used? Obviously, brief strategic intervention is not appropriate for all problem situations. In this chapter we consider when brief strategic intervention should and should not be used.

Modes of working with students demonstrating problem behavior at school fall along a continuum. At one end (and usually tried first) are the simple, commonsense methods of changing behavior—making direct requests for changed behavior, providing specific information and skill-training, or using reinforcement and reward systems. Next are methods focused on changing specific attitudes felt to support particular behaviors. These include problem clarification, persuasion, providing emotional support, or manipulation of feelings. Toward the other end of the continuum are the more intensive psychotherapeutic tactics, such as brief strategic intervention, which focus on changing entrenched beliefs and response patterns. At the far end of the continuum are the long-term, reconstructive individual or family therapies, which are designed to change underlying character and relationship structures.

Normally, simple, straightforward methods of changing student behavior are quite effective. Thus, these methods should be tried first. Only when these straightforward approaches fail to resolve a student's problem should brief strategic or other more intensive psychotherapeutic tactics be considered. Consequently, it always makes sense to assume at first that a student's problem is capable of being resolved in a simple, straightforward manner. If in fact a more intensive mode of intervention is necessary, it will quickly become apparent. For example, if a counselor or teacher assumes that a student's problem is largely one of ignorance or confusion at what is expected of her, and begins by offering information or clarification, it may soon become quite obvious that the student knows or understands what is expected but either chooses not to act on that information or believes, for whatever reason, that she cannot act on that knowledge. This outcome indicates that the student (or someone else) is operating under certain beliefs that prevent her from being able to act on a direct request or suggestion for changed behavior.

At this point, the practitioner may need to consider what might be blocking such a response. There are three possible interpretations: that the person is in such emotional turmoil as a result of some current trauma that she cannot act upon the information, that her current life context is so disorganized as to make it impossible for her to act in a predictable manner, or that specific beliefs about the problem behavior are so entrenched as to make it impossible for her to try anything different.

We all know examples of the first type of situation. A student may be so overwhelmed by events such as the death of a friend or family member, his parents' divorce, relocation to a new community, or parental loss of a job that he is extremely reactive emotionally and unable to function effectively in school. In a situation characterized by intense emotional crisis, interventions that offer a sense of control, structure, stability, and nurturance to the child and his family are much more appropriate than brief strategic methods.

In the second type of situation, certain contexts in which the student exists may be so chronically chaotic as to fail to provide the stability necessary for the child to learn predictable ways of behaving. Typical of this kind of situation would be one in which the parents had abdicated their parenting functions as a result of alcoholism, chronic physical or mental illness, or chronic social and economic deprivation. In such circumstances, it is often difficult for the children to know what to expect from others, such as teachers or parents, and thus impossible to discern what is appropriate behavior. Often, the children are expected to—and do—raise themselves. In these cases, the method of choice would be intensive individual or family-oriented psychotherapeutic efforts aimed at building a more predictable emotional structure for the student, either within or outside of her family.

If we exclude these two types of circumstances, and if student problem behavior is resistant to more direct interventions, then brief strategic methods should be considered. Such methods are particularly appropriate when it is easy to discern that a student's problem behavior is being responded to by others in a persistent and repetitive way at school and/or at home. However, it is sometimes difficult to see how responses aimed at solving a student's problem are inadvertently maintaining it. To increase one's ability to discern such problem-promoting interactions between family members, school staff, and a student demonstrating problems, five common patterns will be described. Fisch, Weakland, and Segal (1982) characterize the five patterns as follows: attempting to force something that can only occur spontaneously, attempting to master a feared event by postponing it, attempting to reach accord through opposition, attempting to obtain compliance through voluntarism, and confirming the accuser's suspicions by attempting to defend oneself.

Central to each of these patterns is a discrepancy between what the situation actually demands and what the person believes is the right way to respond to it. This discrepancy results in a mishandling of the situation and perpetuation of the problem behavior. Because these patterns occur with great regularity in school as well as in life outside of school, we will illustrate through school case examples how these ways of responding are wrong for the particular problem.

The first pattern—attempting to force something that can only occur spontaneously—is seen in situations in which the person reports that his complaint is with himself, not another person. It concerns a problem he has regarding his own functioning, either physical or mental. Problems of physical functioning may involve behaviors such as vomiting, bedwetting, poor bowel functioning, stuttering, or difficulty with breathing, eating, or sleeping. Mental functioning problems may involve problems of mood (depression), obsessions or compulsions, or mental blocks to performance.

It is assumed that all people experience dips in their physical or mental functioning at one time or another. Most people do not get too upset with these dips, and typically the disturbances correct themselves spontaneously in a short time. However, if a person defines such fluctuations as a problem and takes deliberate steps to correct them and prevent their future occurrence, he can become enmeshed in a painful and unworkable problem/solution pattern. The person may try, for example, to force himself to sleep, to not vomit, or to feel happy. Even when methods such as willpower or positive thinking fail to bring about the desired performance, they are often tried again and again, creating an even bigger problem in the mind of the person involved. Take the case of Niki, the little girl described in Chapter One who vomited during lunchtime at school. Embarrassed by the attention this action triggered from her classmates and the school staff, she then worried about the recurrence of the vomiting, getting herself more and more upset. In such a state she vomited again, thus confirming her worst fears. Consequently, even more of her attention was devoted to willing herself not to vomit, trying to coerce a performance from herself that could only occur spontaneously. Others unwittingly escalated the problem. When her teacher and the lunchroom supervisor asked on subsequent days whether she was feeling sick again or whether she thought she might vomit, such well-meant actions caused the child to try even harder not to vomit, which just made things worse. So while this particular pattern may sound like an exclusively individual one, in reality, it is also an interpersonal problem because other people in the person's social context may unwittingly be strengthening the expectation that the particular solution attempted should work.

With this class of problems, solving them becomes much more likely if the student gives up her efforts to coerce herself into a certain performance. However, this cannot be done by simply telling her to stop trying so hard. In the next chapters we will discuss a process that can be used to help a child replace an unworkable solution such as this one.

Another type of vicious-circle pattern Fisch and his associates have observed is associated with problems of performance and involves a child who has some fear or anxiety about his performance in a situation that has not yet occurred. Phobias, shyness, speech blocks, and stage fright all fall into this category. The five-year-old boy's school phobia described below is a typical example of how problems in this category arise and are maintained.

The little boy's fear of attending school started innocently. One day at school the teacher reprimanded another student. The teacher's intensity scared the boy, causing him to anticipate the same happening to him. He dwelt on this thought, making himself more and more upset with questions like, what if the teacher screams at me? What if she makes me do something I can't do? What if I can't get out of this situation if it becomes too embarrassing or risky? These problematic thoughts and feelings became even more intense when the boy was put back in the situation by adults and told, "Of course you can handle it," thus creating the expectation that he should be able to handle it, although he felt he could not.

The boy came to regard the feared event as something he was not ready to master (although everyone else obviously was able to), despite being told by well-meaning adults that it was a simple thing to master. The boy responded to this predicament by deciding to use the solution of mastery by delay: He decided to postpone attending school until he felt he wasn't so scared anymore.

Other situations in which this same type of misguided solution may be followed involve concerns about academic or social performance. The girl who fears how she will perform on a speech before the class will try to put off her speechmaking no matter how much she has rehearsed it until she feels more confident or can figure out a surefire method to get her through. The teenager wanting to ask a certain girl out on a date but fearful of getting turned down will postpone asking anyone for a date. Instead, he will talk about waiting for the right time or learning a guaranteed line from a friend. As Fisch, Weakland, and Segal (1982) note, in each of these situations the person's basic solution is to prepare for the feared event in such a way that the event is mastered in advance. Because one can never really feel she has mastered something not experienced, the feared event is constantly postponed. Regrettably, this solution of preparing for a feared event by postponing it is often reinforced by the well-meant suggestions of others. Trying to assist a student by offering suggestions as to how to prepare more effectively for the situation may often intensify the problem by maintaining the solution of postponement to which the student is wedded. Consequently, while this pattern also may appear to be primarily concerned with the way the individual person is responding, in actuality, the solution behavior is maintained through interpersonal contacts.

In contrast to the above two patterns, in which a person reports some problem concerning his own performance, in the following pattern the problem centers on a person's concern with another's response to him. This concern typically involves a conflict between a student and teacher, a parent and child, two students, or parents and school professionals. Often only one of the two conflicting parties seeks assistance. Usually it is the person who feels that she is not being responded to correctly by the other party. It may be a teacher who feels a student does not respect her authority or a student who feels he has been treated unfairly by a teacher or another student.

An example of this pattern reported by Williams and Weeks (1984) involved an eighth-grade girl who complained about the amount of work being given her by a teacher and her inability to get the work done on time. She also complained about a friend who no longer called her or seemed to want to do things with her. The girl was boiling over with anger and resentment, feeling that she was being treated unfairly by both and that she deserved more attention from them. She responded by continually requesting that the teacher make exceptions for her and constantly phoning her friend. However, these responses only provoked the very behavior from the teacher and friend that the girl wished to eliminate. Rather than becoming more responsive and attentive, they became exasperated with her demands and distanced themselves more from her. Thus the student's demands to be treated one-up only led to being treated one-down.

Because the behaviors asked for in these situations often seem reasonable and fair, it is easy for the practitioner not to recognize that the problem-maintaining aspect of this solution is not *what* is being asked of another, but *how* it is being asked. In these situations, write Fisch, Weakland, and Segal (1982), the person concerned usually attempts to get his expectations about another's treatment of him met through coercion. This may take the form either of overtly haranguing the other party to comply with his demands or silently punishing the other party into submission. Because either method of getting equal treatment results in the other party feeling she is being dictated to, both result in more of the very behavior from the other party that the person is complaining about.

Another pattern is commonly demonstrated when a person would like someone to do something but for some reason feels he cannot ask directly for compliance. This particular contradiction between what a person wants to have happen in a situation and how they operate in that situation can demonstrate itself in a number of adult-child problems. In one such situation reported by Williams and Weeks (1984), a seventh-grade girl was referred to the guidance office because she was leaving her science class almost every day upset. According to the student, the cause of her upset was that she didn't like her science teacher. The girl would meet the guidance counselor in the morning crying and asking permission to leave this class. In a conference with the student and her mother, it was learned that this same situation had occurred the previous year and that the mother had removed her daughter from the upsetting class. The mother indicated that she was very troubled that this was happening again. She reported usually allowing her daughter to join her and calm down rather than forcing her to stay in a class when she was upset. It appeared that the mother was reluctant to ask that her daughter do something she might find distasteful. This response seemed based upon the perception that the daughter was somehow fragile and incapable of determining her own level of tolerance—that she couldn't stay in class rather than that she wouldn't.

Such perceptions of fragility often cause a person to respond to the fragile one with an indirect request. This indirect request is then met by a veiled refusal: It is not that the child refuses to attend class, it is that she can't attend class, because of being upset. Thus the perception of the daughter's condition as fragile is reinforced, and the mother then engages in more indirect or cushioned responses to the daughter. Fisch, Weakland, and Segal (1982, p. 154) characterize the two parts of this particular vicious circle as "I'm not really telling you what I want you to do" and "OK, I'm not really refusing, either." In this situation, one person attempts to gain compliance from another while denying (for a variety of reasons) that compliance is being asked for; in turn, the other party chooses not to comply, yet does not openly reject the request. Each response leads to more of the same response from the other party, thus establishing a vicious circle.

A fifth type of self-perpetuating pattern is commonly established under the following circumstances. One person suspects another of some wrongdoing (for example, being delinquent, taking drugs, or telling lies) and accuses that person. The accused person responds, in turn, by denying the accusations and defending himself. However, this response only serves to make the accuser even surer of her accusations—after all, if he were not guilty, why would he react so strongly? This, in turn, triggers the accused to become even stronger in defending himself, which triggers the accuser to become even more suspicious. Thus, the cycle goes on, ad infinitum.

An interesting illustration of this pattern reported by Papp (1983) involved a fifteen-year-old girl who constantly accused her mother of being a bad mother. The parents had divorced several years earlier, and the girl constantly blamed her mother for the divorce, for having robbed her of her father, for having neglected her and her brother by going back to work, and for her latest crime, getting engaged to a man whom the daughter disapproved of because he smoked. These charges made the mother feel guilty, and she responded by constantly trying to appease her daughter, believing this was the only way she could redeem herself. She went to all sorts of extremes in doing this, waiting on her hand and foot and lavishing gifts on her. Regrettably, these efforts at defending herself had an effect opposite to the one she intended. The more she would do for the girl, the more surly and accusing the daughter would become. Finally the mother would explode and either swear at or hit the girl. Then the daughter would point an accusing finger, having proven that she was a bad mother. Watzlawick, Weakland, and Fisch (1974) refer to this interactional pattern as the game of accuser/defender. It can be observed in school-related problems ("I'm sure he's cheating on tests"), home-related problems ("We know he's taking drugs"), and work-related difficulties ("I know she can't control her class").

In each of these five vicious-circle patterns, the particular solution behavior applied actually triggers more of the problem behavior. In trying to determine why such solution behaviors actually provoke the problem behavior and keep it going, it is important to compare the actual nature of the problem situation with what the people involved believe is the nature of that situation—that is, their solution frame. In the first pattern described above, for example, in which an individual attempts to force a performance from herself, the problem is the attempt to apply a solution frame that fits *voluntary* behavior to a situation in which *involuntary* behavior is in question. Due to this mismatch, a nonresolvable cycle is initiated. Similarly, when a problematic behavior is framed as involuntary when it is, in fact, under voluntary control (such as in attempting to gain compliance through voluntarism), a wrong solution is applied that triggers even more of the problem behavior.

In summary, these vicious-circle patterns can maintain many different kinds of persistent student problems. Once the school practitioner learns how to discern the problem and the pattern in which it is embedded, he can begin to consider effective ways of interrupting the pattern. As a first step in this process, the practitioner must decide with whom to work. In the next chapter, this intervention issue is discussed in detail.

CHAPTER 4

Managing the Change Process

In the brief strategic approach, the initiative for change is taken by the school helping professional. It is the helping professional, not the person reporting the problem, who is responsible for managing the change process—deciding with whom to work, framing a solvable problem, setting goals, designing interventions to achieve those goals, correcting such interventions on an as-needed basis, and evaluating the intervention's effectiveness. This does not mean that the practitioner ignores the wishes and expectations of those involved. Rather, he needs to be acutely aware of and responsive to the needs and expectations of such people. However, it is the practitioner who must decide how to proceed rather than the people reporting the problem.

In deciding how to intervene, it is important first to listen carefully to those reporting the problem in order to determine how people view the problem, with whom they believe the practitioner should work, and what they propose should be done to resolve the problem. These various types of information reveal the frame in which people view the problem and attempt to resolve it, and the terms under which they expect help to be provided. The practitioner needs to deter-

Note: Portions of this chapter are excerpted from Amatea, E. "Engaging the Reluctant Client: Some New Strategies for the School Counselor," *The School Counselor,* 1988, *36,* 34–40. Reprinted here by permission of AACD Publishers.

mine whether this frame and set of terms are too limiting for problem solving to proceed effectively. If this is so, the practitioner needs to construct a more workable frame and terms by shifting the expectations of those involved.

Each of these steps is essential for effectively managing the change effort. In this chapter, I describe each of these—examining the initial terms under which help is expected, deciding when these initial terms are too limiting, and redefining them when necessary. Finally, I discuss particular external and internal role expectations that may hamper a school practitioner's attempts to resolve student problems effectively.

Frequently, school practitioners do not consider they have actually begun to intervene in resolving a student's problem until they have met with the student demonstrating the problem. In the brief strategic approach, however, preliminary contacts made with those reporting a student problem (for example, a discussion over coffee in the teacher's lounge, or a brief phone call from a parent) are considered an integral part of the intervention process because they reveal the frame in which such persons perceive the student's problem and try to resolve it. Such contacts also reveal their expectations as to how the practitioner is to proceed in resolving the problem. For example, when a teacher has a concern about a student and explains that concern to a school helping professional, the teacher takes a particular perspective on the problem. That perspective is based on certain assumptions about children, teaching, learning, and so on. The teacher also has expectations about how to proceed most effectively to solve the student's problem or work with others in doing so. Examining these terms and determining whether they are too narrow for intervention to proceed effectively is of central importance in effectively managing the change effort.

How does one identify the initial terms proposed? Whether it be through a teacher's lengthy discussion of a student or a cryptic message from the principal that a child needs special help, all initial contacts about a student's problem contain implicit terms that organize the school practitioner's definition of the student's problem and how it should be solved. For example, who is defined as the person needing help? Is it the person reporting the problem or someone else? How is it expected that the problem should be solved? How should the school helping professional function in solving the problem? Consider how the following statement made to the school psychologist by a third-grade teacher reveals the teacher's implicit definition of the problem, how the problem is to be solved, and how the psychologist is to intervene: "Bobby really needs to see someone. He just won't settle down and do his work. All he wants to do is talk to people, play, or catch someone's attention. And while he's doing that, he's stopping others from getting their work done. The only way he gets anything done is for me to constantly be on his back. I have to watch him and keep an eye on him all the time. He's just got to learn that he needs to settle down and get to work. Can you help him with this?"

This teacher defines the problem as one that rests in Bobby rather than in anyone else (herself included). In addition, her comment reveals that the major thrust of all of her efforts to deal with this problem have been to make Bobby settle down and do his work. Her comment also reveals her expectations about how the psychologist should provide help. In this regard, the teacher expects the psychologist to work with Bobby in a way similar to her own, "[getting him] to learn that he needs to settle down and get to work." Thus, this initial request for help reveals implicit definitions of who has the problem, how the problem is to be solved, and how the change agent is to intervene. In addition, as can be seen here, these requests for help typically direct the practitioner to solve the problem using the same type of solution as has been applied before.

Usually, these terms for help are influenced more by who is reporting the problem than by some absolute reality in the problem situation. For example, another teacher talking about the same third grader described the situation quite differently: "I am at my wit's end in trying to keep Bobby on task. He's one of the brightest students in the class, but he just can't seem to settle down and focus on a task. He is so easily distracted by other children and other things. I have to make sure he's followed through on each task I give him. But I have too much else to do to be so tied down to reminding him to get on task all the time. I need to find some different ways to work with him. Could we talk about what I could do?"

This statement is not just a different phrasing of the same problem. This teacher has a different view of the problem and what must be done to resolve it. Although referring to the same problem student, this teacher defines the problem as one involving her and her ability to work with Bobby. Not only does her request for help contain a statement as to who is in need of help, it also defines what type of help she expects. In contrast to the first teacher, this teacher expects the solution to the problem to lie in her finding a more effective way of working with Bobby. She, rather than Bobby, is to learn a different way of behaving. Her statement also reflects her expectations as to how the psychologist should function to bring this about. The teacher, rather than Bobby, is to work with the psychologist.

As these two examples illustrate, while all initial requests for help contain particular perspectives defining who has the problem and how the practitioner is to solve this problem, competing views may be represented. In deciding which perspective to accept or modify, the practitioner must consider how much the terms implied in such a perspective limit her ability to resolve the problem effectively and make her own decision concerning whom to work with.

To manage the change effort effectively, the practitioner must not only identify the initial terms under which help is sought, but also decide whether these terms are too limiting. For example, the practitioner must decide with whom he considers it is best to work. Second, he must decide how best to intervene to resolve the presenting problem. Deciding whom to work with is best done after determining who is involved in the complaint. For example, is more than one person involved? A teacher, for example, may report a problem with two students in her classroom who constantly bicker with each other. This problem, then, involves both the teacher and the students. Thus, figuring out how many people are involved in the problem or complaint is the first step in managing the change effort.

Determining who is most interested in resolving the problem is the second step. Often the practitioner is expected to work with individuals who only come to see her under duress. Even if a person is not committed to getting help but only comes because he is forced to, the practitioner may be able to interest him in receiving help. If not, the person who sought the change effort may be involved. Although most people expect that the person about whom a problem is reported should be the one with whom the practitioner works, often it is more useful to work with someone else—someone who is more discomfited by the problem and thus more interested in resolving it. In brief strategic intervention, it is assumed that altering the behavior of any individual in a system can influence the behavior of other members of that system. Consequently, the person reporting the most apparent discomfort with the problem behavior can often be involved in the change effort with excellent results.

As a rule of thumb, therefore, if the person demonstrating the problem is not particularly interested in resolving her problem despite efforts to involve her, and there is another person discomfited by the problem, that second person may be the best one for the practitioner to work with. For example, consider the case of Scott described in Chapter Two. If you recall, the practitioner chose to work with Scott's mother and father rather than with Scott. This was a deliberate decision based on the counselor's observation that Scott's parents were much more concerned about his lack of academic achievement than Scott was and thus more motivated to follow the counselor's directives.

After gathering this information, the practitioner must consider what would be the most effective way to intervene. Often, the practitioner may decide that the problem can be solved more quickly or effectively by working in a manner different from what is expected by those seeking help. For example, two middle school boys were embroiled constantly in disputes that each complained the other had started. The teacher finally referred them to the school counselor's office after her efforts to resolve the problem (by explaining that their fighting would not be tolerated, warning them they would be sent to the principal's office, and then sending them there several times) had failed. In referring the two boys to the counselor, the teacher expected the counselor to meet with the two boys together, explore what had happened, and in some way direct them to stop fighting. It quickly became apparent to the counselor, however, that the boys would continue fighting with each other even in her office. Consequently, the counselor decided to meet with the two students individually rather than jointly. By meeting with each student alone, she could work on winning the cooperation of each boy and suggest actions that each student could take in relation to the other. If she had been limited to meeting with both boys together, she would have had to be careful not to take sides with either. This would have significantly limited what she could propose and the range of rationales she could offer to each boy to win his cooperation. Furthermore, because the practitioner will often want to suggest that one of the parties take certain actions that will have a deliberate effect on the other party, it is important to feel free to work with the conflicting parties separately if necessary. Thus, when help is requested, the practitioner must evaluate each situation in terms of these three questions. If the practitioner decides to modify the original terms proposed, special tactics may be needed to shift the thinking of those involved.

Sometimes, the person who reports a problem may readily agree to a different approach to resolving a problem when a logical explanation is provided. More often than not, however, people may be reluctant to shift their expectations as to how a problem is to be solved. This is not because they are stubborn or inherently resistant. People often cling to their own ideas as to how a problem should be resolved more out of caution than anything else. Their way seems the only safe and sane thing to do given the current circumstances. In such instances, shifting the ideas of those involved takes special care and attention. Two very different types of brief strategic tactics commonly used in such situations are soft-sell and hard-sell (Rosenthal and Bergman, 1986). Soft-sell tactics, such as accepting and extending a person's original ideas or preempting a person's resistance, are often used when it appears that the person with whom one is interacting is receptive to one's influence but needs to be motivated to follow a particular shift in direction. In contrast, hard-sell tactics, such as undermining the person's position or emphasizing the dangers of improvement, are typically used when the person with whom one is interacting demonstrates limited compliance with or trust in one's leadership.

Rather than directly clashing with a person's ideas about the nature of a problem or its solution, the practitioner can accept his ideas, and then extend them further than originally considered. Saposnek (1980) suggests using the person's own language and values to extend his ideas further than he had considered doing. This might be called a "Yes, and" in contrast to a "Yes, but" technique. The following situation demonstrates the use of this type of method by a school social worker. The teacher has requested that the social worker meet with an eighth-grade girl who has not responded to the teacher's straightforward efforts to help the girl stop crying in his class. Because the teacher's description of the problem situation indicates a strong possibility that the girl will not be motivated to work on her problem with the social worker, this practitioner may decide that the teacher is the person with whom she should work to resolve the girl's problem. In implementing such a decision, however, the social worker needs to shift the teacher to considering how he could be involved in the change effort. The following exchange illustrates how the social worker's attempts to accept and extend the teacher's ideas are designed to restructure the teacher's expectations for involvement in the change effort.

Teacher: Sara's been having a lot of trouble in my class. She has cried every day for the last three weeks, and yet when I attempt to talk with her she just shuts me out.

Social Worker: What do you think is happening with her?

Teacher: I really don't know. She won't talk to me. I've tried to be understanding, but I can't seem to get her to open up at all. I'd like to help her, but I just can't seem to get through to her. While I am concerned about her, I just can't have her crying. The other students have begun to be upset by her behavior, and things seem to be getting worse. I finally told her she just has to come see you to do something about her crying. She agreed that she would come, and I wanted to let you know I was sending her down to your office.

Social Worker: I'll be glad to see Sara, but before I set up an appointment, let me first ask, How interested do you think Sara is in seeing me?

Teacher: Well, I've been encouraging her to see you for some time now, but she balked at the idea. But yesterday she spent the entire period just crying to herself quietly. I tried talking with her after class awhile, and I think I finally got through to her that something had to be done. She said she would come if I arranged it with you.

Social Worker: I see. Well, she seems like she may not be too motivated, doesn't she? I'm not sure how much she will follow through. You know, we might save time in the long run if I could meet with you at least once and find out more about Sara. Even more, you and I might be able to think of some ways to get her to be more motivated to seek help or to use it.

Although the teacher revealed in his first statement that he regarded Sara as the person with the problem, he also identified that he was more discomfited by Sara's problem than was Sara herself. Thus the teacher, not Sara, appears to be the one most wanting the situation to change. As we mentioned earlier, this may often be the best person with whom to work. Thus, the social worker may decide that the best approach would be to meet with the teacher and learn more about Sara's problem behavior and the teacher's current solution efforts.

The social worker can avert a number of difficulties by taking this tack rather than simply agreeing with the teacher's request to see the student. First, since the student's motivation is questionable, chances are she will not be too cooperative if she shows up at all. Second, the intervention will have begun under the terms that the girl is to be cured while the teacher waits passively for her to improve. If the social worker waits until a later time to meet with the teacher, she might encounter even greater resistance from the teacher about shifting the terms of who is to be involved. This is because the teacher would have been allowed to view the problem and its solution as separate from himself, and so would see the social worker's delayed invitation for him to participate as a sign of failure on the practitioner's part to reach the girl. Instead of limiting her options as to how she will work, the social worker can offer the teacher the alternative of being included in the intervention process from the very beginning. If the teacher agrees to this arrangement, he will also have agreed implicitly to being involved in the intervention, rather than simply standing by.

But what if the teacher resists this idea? In such a case, the social worker need not insist that he come in. Instead, she can appear to agree while accomplishing the same end. For example, she might say, "All right, if you think that might be best. Have Sara come in. However, since you indicated that her motivation is somewhat lukewarm, don't be surprised if she refuses at the last minute. If she does, don't make an issue of her coming in. Instead, you can say that you are planning to come in anyway without her, so that she can see how serious is your concern about her." But what if the teacher still insists that the student be seen alone? For example, he might state, "I just know she won't really open up if I am there. I'll come in another time if necessary." Again the social worker need not insist that the teacher come in either with or without the girl. Instead, she can graciously agree to the teacher's request but then put the responsibility for the outcome of the venture on him. For example, she might say, "All right, I can see why you are thinking that way, and I will be glad to make an appointment for her. But, you do need to know that often when a youngster is questionably motivated, as it seems Sara is, it rarely works out to start with the student. But I trust your judgment and hope that she will use this opportunity to get help. If she does, fine. If I see that she is just going through the motions, though, I'll be sure to tell you, as we may need to meet together to decide what to do. Anyhow, there's no need to worry about it now; let's just see how it goes." If the student turns out to want the social worker's help, all is well. However, if the student resists the social worker's help, the social worker is still in an influential position since the student has proved her correct. Thus she may then be able to enlist the teacher's help more readily.

In each of these moves, the social worker agrees with but then extends the teacher's original ideas concerning how the problem is to be solved. Obviously, this method of shifting expectations depends on the practitioner not getting pressured to perform, taking her time, and knowing that everything does not have to be resolved right away, as time is on her side.

Another tactic used to sell a new point of view about how the problem should be solved involves preempting a person's resistance to a proposed shift. One way of doing this is to anticipate what the person's negative reactions might be to a new idea (that is, their reasons for resisting the idea) and then express these ideas in a more extreme form. For example, let us say the teacher who referred Sara to the social worker for help has continued to hope that Sara's class behavior will improve. The social worker, however, has met with the girl, and the student has clearly indicated she is not interested in working on her problem. Rather than feel at a dead end, the social worker can decide to involve the teacher in responding differently to Sara. To motivate the teacher to be more involved in the change effort and increase his readiness to accept the social worker's suggestions for dealing differently with Sara, the social worker could first reemphasize the seriousness of the situation with which the teacher is contending. Since this is something the teacher has been saying all along in various ways, one would assume he would agree with this idea. Next, the social worker could state that it appeared quite clear that the teacher himself was the only one sufficiently concerned and influential to be in a position to give Sara the help she needed so much—not her parents, nor other school personnel, nor even the social worker. Finally, the social worker could point out that even though he was the only one in a position to really help the girl, it was certainly understandable if he decided to just wash his hands of Sara, since she had given him such a hard time. After all, he had many other students to attend to, and the year would end after a time, and he could put Sara behind him. With this tactic, the typical reasons for the teacher backing away from involvement in the change effort are openly stated by the social worker, but in such a way that the teacher may find them hard to agree with. These comments thus serve to disarm the teacher's natural resistance to becoming more involved.

Another way to preempt a person's resistance to following the school practitioner's lead consists of having the practitioner take a one-down position. For example, the social worker in Sara's case might preface a proposal for the teacher to consider a different tack with statements such as "I'm not sure this will help, but . . ." or "You are probably going to think that I am a little nuts, but have you considered. . . ." By this method, the practitioner seeks to disarm the natural resistance a person often experiences to being told what to do by someone else.

Both accepting and extending ideas and preempting the client's resistance are considered soft-sell tactics. They are designed to increase the person's compliance with the practitioner's point of view through gentle influence and redirection. In some instances, however, the person with whom one is working will demonstrate an attitude of little trust and cooperation over and over again. In these instances, hard-sell tactics may be required. Unlike soft-sell tactics, hard-sell tactics encourage the person to defy the change agent and thereby move the person in a direction the practitioner considers necessary for problem resolution to occur. Two such defiance-inducing tactics are emphasizing the dangers of improvement and undermining the person's position.

When a person has consistently demonstrated resistance to following the practitioner's lead, it may be preferable to move in the opposite direction, emphasizing the dangers inherent in resolving the problem. This tactic banks on the person defying the practitioner's request not to change. To do this, the practitioner asked the person to consider the drawbacks to improving the problem situation. (Note that the practitioner does not ask *if* there would be any drawbacks.) Most of the time, the person will reply that there are no dangers and that resolving the problem would be immensely better. The practitioner must then describe a possible drawback to improvement—if not for the person with the problem, then for someone close to him. Providing even one credible drawback can justify the practitioner's position that it could be dangerous to improve the problem situation.

Instead of exhorting someone to follow a particular line of thinking or action, the practitioner may choose to agree with her that changing her present position is inadvisable—but for reasons that are unpalatable to the person involved. This move undermines the person's ideas about her original position. For example, a practitioner might describe how much the person's opponent would gain if she didn't change her present response to the problem situation. Another approach might be to describe how much the person's opponent might suffer if the person *did* change her position. A delightful example illustrating the use of this latter approach was provided in a case reported by Watzlawick, Weakland, and Fisch (1974, p. 138). It involved a teenage boy who was suspended from school after he had been caught selling drugs on the school grounds. According to Watzlawick and his associates, when news reached the boy of his suspension from school, the boy reacted with annoyance, not because he would miss school, but because his suspension would cut deeply into the profits from his drug dealing.

[The boy's] annoyance became intense anger when the principal told him that the suspension was "for his own good and to help him." While he was to be suspended, the principal informed him, he would be given credit for any work he did on his own at home—homework assignments, preparing for examinations, etc.—and his mother would be allowed to pick up these assignments at school and bring them home to him. Since the boy had not been much of a student to begin with, but now was furious with the principal over the suspension, he announced to his mother that he would be damned if he would do any schoolwork. It was at this point that the mother sought help.

Her hope was that the therapist could get the boy into his office and somehow make him accept the principal's ruling so that he would not remain so angry and therefore intransigent about schoolwork. Instead, the therapist, realizing that the boy's anger with the principal afforded a lever for change, instructed the mother as follows: She was to go home and simply tell the boy that she had talked over his situation with some other mothers and had come to realize something, but that she was not sure whether she should tell him what it was. After some brief hesitation she was to go ahead and come out with this troublesome "realization": that his principal was noted for stressing the importance of students attending classes, that he believed quite firmly that a student just could not keep up with his studies without faithful attendance, and that he had probably suspended him to make him fail the entire school year. She was then to point out to the boy that if during his suspension from school he should do as well [as] or even better on his own than when he attended class, the principal would be very red-faced and embarrassed. She was to finish this narrative by suggesting that it might be for the best if he did not "do too well," and thereby save the principal's face. The mother subsequently reported to the therapist that when he heard this, her son's face lit up with a diabolical grin and revenge shone in his eyes. He had found a way to gain retribution, and it mattered little that it would require his buckling down to work. In a follow-up session the mother reported that her son had thrown himself into his schoolwork "with a vengeance" and was beginning to get better grades than ever before.

While this may seem an unconventional and even unprincipled change tactic, it reflects the way in which the degree of resistance demonstrated is considered in selecting an appropriate tactic. Individuals who demonstrate strong resistance to any direct efforts to influence them to change their actions or attitudes, such as the boy described above, often require tactics that use their oppositional stance in the service of change.

Typically the process of deciding whether to use soft-sell or hard-sell tactics consists of first trying more gentle soft-sell tactics to shift the original terms of the problem. Only after trying these and noting that the person involved consistently resists such methods should the practitioner turn to hard-sell tactics. In the following example, a school counselor has been asked by a boy's parents to help their sixteen-year-old son, Philip, who refuses to attend school. The youngster is now in the counselor's office, but only in response to duress from his parents. The central issue facing the counselor here is that of deciding whom to involve in the change effort. While the parents assume the youngster should be the one involved, the fact that the student does not appear interested means the counselor must first consider whether she can motivate the student to become more interested in the change effort. Rather than push hard at getting the student to see his need for help—and risk becoming exasperated by his lack of interest—the counselor might use one of the following tactics suggested by Fisch, Weakland, and Segal (1982): renegotiating the problem, bringing in the person most discomfited by the problem, or undermining the student's position. These tactics differ in terms of how the leverage for change is applied. The first two are soft-sell tactics, while the latter is a hard-sell tactic. As demonstrated in the following case excerpts, each of these tactics can be tried in the order in which they are presented here, with the practitioner moving on only when the preceding one fails.

As Fisch, Weakland, and Segal (1982, p. 40) put it, "Some people who seek help under duress from others do want to make some change in a problem or complaint; however, it is not the one for which they were referred. For these individuals it may be possible to negotiate a different problem to be worked on." Therefore, as a first step in dealing with Philip, the counselor can offer him an opportunity to register his own complaint as a possible focus for a change effort.

Counselor: OK. So if I hear you right, your mom and dad are making a big fuss about you going to school and graduating, but as far as you are concerned it's really no problem. And if it weren't for the flap they are making, you probably wouldn't even be here.

Philip: Yeah, they think the world has come to an end now that I won't go to school. That there's no hope for me. I think they mean business about turning me over to the juvenile authorities if I don't go to school.

Counselor: That sounds like a pretty strong reaction they are having. I can sure see how you might be rattled about it, but I'd feel funny working with you on going to school if that is something which is not a problem to you. I'd rather spend my time working on something that is meaningful to you, not just to your mom and dad. So let me ask you this: Is there any other kind of problem you've been struggling with which really does bother you; maybe something which you have had in mind doing something about but always put off?

Philip: Well, I don't know if this is the kind of thing you work on. Oh, hell, I might as well say it. I just don't know anybody at that school. I try to talk to people and make friends, but somehow nothing works. It's just miserable going there. I just hate it.

Counselor: And this bugs you a lot more than skipping school or graduating?

Philip: Yeah. Do you work with that kind of thing?

Philip has offered a renegotiated complaint. He is interested not in working on the problem of his school attendance, but in doing something about his social situation. While the counselor does not have to commit to working on just that problem (for example, the school attendance problem can be dealt with in the context of his social situation), giving Philip an opportunity to come forth with his own complaint has made it much more likely that she will be able to work with him at all.

The following dialogue illustrates a somewhat different version of this same approach that can be tried if the student does not come up with a problem he wishes to work on. In this tactic, the counselor suggests an alternate problem that is rather undeniable—that the student is being hassled to seek counseling.

Counselor: OK, so you don't feel you really have any problem that is bothering you or that needs attention in counseling. But you do have one problem.

Philip: What is that?

Counselor: Well, you still have your mom and dad on your back, right? They're the ones who are making you come in here, and they're not likely to just give up at one session.

Philip: Humph!

Counselor: You may not be interested in working on what your mom and dad think is important, but would you be interested in getting them off your back?

Philip: Yeah, I'd be interested in that.

If the client agrees to this different complaint, it does not mean that the counselor is restricted to that being his primary goal. However, it may allow the counselor to get a foot in the door by dealing with difficulties of more relevance to the student.

Another direction that can be taken in working with reluctant clients involves working with the person who initiates the change effort. Because a problem is viewed in the brief strategic approach as being maintained or escalated by interactions between the identified problem person and others caught up in the problem, the behavior of any of the people involved can be the target of the practitioner's change effort. Consequently, if the person in the practitioner's office seems unconcerned about the problem and another person appears quite put out by it (as in the following example), the practitioner might consider shifting to working with the person pressing the identified client to seek help.

Counselor: From the way you talk, it sounds like the only thing that is really bothering you is the hassle your mom and dad are making about your attending school.

Philip: Yeah, they are really on my case.

Counselor: And other than their hassling you, everything would be all right?

Philip: Yeah, right. I wish they'd just back off.

Counselor: Well, I'd really not want to waste our time doing something that isn't a problem for you. It would be a waste for both of us. If they're making such a big fuss over such a small thing, then the only thing that seems to make sense is if I could see them and maybe help them take it easy a bit more about your skipping school. Would you be interested in that?

Philip: What d'ya mean?

Counselor: Well, I can see if I can't help you get them to relax a bit about this school thing so that they're not hassling you so much.

Philip: Sure. I wouldn't mind that.

The counselor would then call the parents, set up an appointment to see them alone, and begin as with any case by asking, "What's the problem? How have you been trying to deal with it? What specific thing would you like to see changed? What small goal would meet your ideas about how things should be changed?" Since the parents are very likely to view the son as the one who needs to see the counselor, it will be necessary to give an explanation that would make this invitation more acceptable. For example, "Could you meet with me, at least once, to help me understand your son's problem more fully?"

In some cases it may be impossible or inappropriate to call in the person most distressed by the problem, and the student may not offer a renegotiated problem. These circumstances may indicate the need to use a hard-sell tactic to get the change effort under way. Undermining the person's position is one such tactic. It involves getting the student to change his mind about being involved in the change effort by having the school practitioner agree with his no-involvement position, but for reasons that make the position less acceptable. The practitioner would take the position of agreeing with the client that involvement was probably inadvisable but for reasons that were unacceptable to the client, as in the following example.

Counselor: You know, I've been listening to you talk about your dad. He really seems to be on your case, doesn't he?

Philip: Yeah, he's constantly on my back. There's not a thing I do right according to him.

Counselor: It sounds like you have to take a lot of heat from him.

Philip: Yeah, he's just a constant critic. Always so negative! I've heard him tell my mom that he thinks I'm just no good, a "bad seed," he said.

Counselor: So not only does he think you are not going to amount to much, now he's got your mom convinced?

Philip: Well, I don't think she's convinced yet. He's the real butthole.

Counselor: You know, I've been listening to you talk about your dad, and it has just dawned on me what the real reason is that you've been skipping school.

Philip: Huh?

Counselor: You know your dad real well, don't you?

Philip: What do you mean?

Counselor: You know that he really has decided that you are hopeless, that you won't amount to anything, and you know how important it is for him to be right, don't you? I mean, it would just upset him no end if he was wrong, wouldn't it?

Philip: Well, he is stubborn.

Counselor: And so I can see why you've decided not to come to school. Because if you did come, I am rather certain he would become very upset.

Philip: I don't understand.

Counselor: I never realized how much you cared for him. You would screw up your chances of making it after high school to avoid embarrassing him by proving he made a mistake about you. You must really care for him a lot to let him prove he's right about you.

Philip: Me? Sacrifice myself for him? No way!

Counselor: But that's what you have been doing, isn't it? Whether you recognize it consciously or not, your continuing to play deadbeat about school is really making your dad right about you. You're doing an excellent job of making sure he's not suffering the embarrassment of being proven dead wrong. That really is thoughtful of you.

Philip: You've got it all wrong!

Counselor: That's what you say, but you and I know what you really are trying to do. Boy, I never knew you cared for him that much!

Noting the anger the boy showed toward his father, the counselor chose to suggest how much the father would be disadvantaged by the boy doing something about his situation (that is, attending school). Consequently, the counselor agreed with the student's position of not attending school—but for a reason that was unsettling to the student, thereby undermining the student's view of the reason he was not attending school. This reframing of the student's motives as something opposite to what he intended can often result in the student attempting to convince the counselor why it is in his best interest to do something different regarding his problem.

To the school practitioner unfamiliar with brief strategic intervention, these tactics may appear strange or manipulative. They are designed, however, to free the student and school helping professional from the coercive terms in which the change effort has been initiated. To be used effectively, however, certain conditions must be met. First, the practitioner must carefully observe how a person reports on her problem and those attempting to help her solve the problem. Second, the practitioner should observe how the referring person describes both the problem person and his own efforts to help her. These two pieces of information are necessary to assess the degree of coercion and opposition that exists around both the intervention context and the problem behavior. Given this information, the practitioner can select a change tactic based on the degree of opposition noted.

In each of these approaches the practitioner must be careful to separate herself from the focus of the referred person's opposition—the referring person. To do this, the practitioner must give the student the message that she is on the student's side rather than on the referring person's side. While each of the tactics described above gives this message, the tactics obviously differ in terms of the extent to which defiance is used to build client motivation. The first approach described represents a straightforward invitation to be involved in the change effort, while the last one describes an effort to use the client's oppositional stance to motivate him to move away from a particular position. In addition, the school practitioner must be genuine in her concern for the referred person's welfare. These tactics cannot be used effectively if they are delivered with sarcasm or saccharine sweetness. In summary, although the student under duress to seek counseling may or may not feel his problem is serious, the practitioner dealing with him often does. The tactics described here seek to increase the array of options the practitioner has to begin an intervention on more workable terms.

Setting one's own terms for problem solving can seem risky. The practitioner often runs up against commonsense expectations as to how a student's problem should be solved. In addition, the practitioner's own beliefs about how he should function can restrict the range of options he allows himself. Because this approach challenges many of the external and internal role expectations under which the school practitioner routinely operates, it is essential that he be aware of how such expectations can limit his options to intervene.

Several expectations held by both the educational establishment (that is, the principal, teachers, and other school staff) and the larger community can constrain one's freedom to set more workable terms for problem solving. Three such expectations are that the school practitioner be responsible for making students change, always do what is reasonable and logical, and always act fairly and equitably.

While the practitioner does have a responsibility for designing interventions to bring about a change in a student's problem behavior, she is not responsible for making a student change. To take on such a responsibility severely limits her leverage and influence by involving her in power struggles with the person who is deemed to need changing. This role expectation is often delivered in subtle ways and can take the form of pressuring the practitioner to perform in some way. For example, desperate to resolve an ongoing behavior problem with a student, other school professionals may urge the school counselor to do something right away. If the practitioner is to make effective intervention decisions, it is important that they be neither hurried nor premature, and that they not be made before enough is known about what is needed.

In the long run, the practitioner performs a greater service to all concerned if she protects her option to take her time to think carefully and plan what is needed. Thus, one must always be sensitive to being put under pressure, and not hesitate to signal when more time is needed.

A second common role expectation is that the practitioner should always operate in reasonable and logical ways. Because the success of many brief strategic tactics is based on working against common sense and in unexpected ways, such tactics may appear incomprehensible to other school staff members and to parents. In addition, the practitioner runs the risk of someone complaining or becoming irritated when asked to try something new and seemingly illogical.

Further limiting one's intervention choices is the expectation that the practitioner should always be fair—that is, always treat each student fairly and equally. Interestingly, being fair is often defined more by what is usually done than by some impartial standard of justice. Often, in challenging a particular solution that is not working for a student, one also challenges a normative standard of fair behavior. However, because each student is different, what may motivate one to behave differently may not work for another. In order to use brief strategic methods, it is often necessary for the practitioner to free herself from common standards of fairness and equality.

Professional conduct as a school practitioner is often measured in terms of being fair, loving, logical, and responsible. However, in carrying out an intervention designed to move someone to a new behavior, the practitioner's own behavior may appear illogical and be judged irresponsible by others. To increase the freedom needed to move in unexpected ways, the practitioner often finds it necessary to build a base of support first by creating such an expectation in the minds of key school personnel.

At the same time, the practitioner may find it hard to give herself permission to move beyond expected helping behavior. To not always be predictable and understandable is sometimes very difficult. One of the best ways to deal with one's own personal constraints is to take time with new ideas and tactics and not feel pressured to try them out too soon.

In summary, the terms in which help is asked for can often impede the ability of the school practitioner to work effectively. In addition, particular external and internal expectations for performance can restrict his ability to respond. Knowing when such terms are affecting his ability to solve a student problem is important to getting work under way. Next we consider the types of information the practitioner needs to gather about the problem/solution cycle to determine how to proceed in problem solving.

CHAPTER 5

Gathering Information About the Problem/Solution Cycle

To devise an intervention to resolve a persistent student problem, the practitioner must develop a clear picture of the interactional cycle in which the problem behavior and the various behaviors that function to maintain it are embedded. To do this, information must be gathered about the nature of the problem or complaint, how the problem is being handled, what is expected from the intervention, and the language and beliefs of those involved. In this chapter, common methods for gathering information about the first three of these four areas are described, and, in the following chapter, methods for learning about the fourth area are considered.

In all forms of child-focused intervention, information is gathered about the nature of the problem. However, the type of information about the problem sought by brief strategic practitioners is quite different from that collected by practitioners of other schools of thought. In brief strategic intervention, emphasis is placed on developing a picture of the sequence of events around the problem's occurrence (that is, what action follows what other action) and the circumstances in which the problem is demonstrated (that is, where, when, how often, with whom, how much, and so on). Consequently, the practitioner must solicit a behavioral account of specific instances of the problem behavior's occurrence and of people's response to it. Rather than securing a general description of the problem behavior (for example, "Tommy has a

78

hard time listening to and following directions"), a person's response to the problem behavior (for example, "He has to have me work with him for him to get anything done"), or an inferred explanation of the problem behavior (for example, "Tommy seems more immature than the other children in his class"), the practitioner must get a play-by-play account of specific instances of the problem behavior.

This approach to problem clarification typically requires a major shift in focus for most school helping professionals. Despite the fact that school helping professionals usually have an incredible array of sources of information about students, it is often possible to miss obtaining information about the transactional sequence or context in which a problem behavior is embedded. This is because school practitioners (for example, counselors, psychologists, and social workers) as well as parents and other members of the school staff typically have been trained to look at the individual student's behavior to become informed about a problem rather than at the circumstances in which the student's problem behavior occurs. To develop a base of information about the interactional context of a problem behavior, the school practitioner must solicit reports of current instances of the problem. These reports must be precise, detailed, behaviorally oriented accounts of both the problem behavior's occurrence and people's efforts to resolve it.

Brief strategic practitioners (Fisch, Weakland, and Segal, 1982; Weakland, Fisch, Watzlawick, and Bodin, 1974) suggest that the practitioner begin this information-gathering process by inquiring about the problem and how it is being handled. To do this, the school practitioner inquires how the problem-bearer and those involved with her are responding to the problem behavior as it is currently demonstrated. For example, a student's parents or members of the school staff can often provide excellent information as to how a student's problem is being perceived and responded to. However, because most people have been trained to provide a history of a problem—describing its occurrence in the past rather than the present—it is easy to find oneself hearing a long history of the problem rather than an account of its current status. Even though some information about the persistence of the problem is often useful, learning about how the problem is currently being perceived and responded to should be the primary focus of the practitioner's information-gathering efforts. Consequently, if the practitioner finds herself listening to a great deal of history, she may want to suggest that the current status of the problem needs to be investigated first. This might be done by saying, for example, "You know, I think I might understand better by hearing about how the problem is occurring now. After that, we can look backwards in time. So tell me how you see the problem happening now?" This does not need to be a contested process, however. If people are determined to tell about their past history with a problem, it is certainly acceptable to just listen patiently and gather information about the problem's current operation afterwards.

Brief strategic practitioners usually begin gathering information about the problem with a general question such as "What do you see as the problem?" or "What is the problem that brings you here?" To become informed about the interactional context surrounding a problem behavior (that is, how the behavior is being responded to by the problem-bearer and others), the practitioner must move beyond general questions toward more specific ones that provide detailed information about who is doing what to whom. Specific questions—such as Where and when does the problem occur? How often? How much? What happens first? What about after that? And then what happens? What is said and done by whom to whom, when, where, and how?—help to shape a picture of the sequence of events and the circumstances around the problem behavior's occurrence. Of course, the practitioner does not deluge people with these questions all at once. Instead, she addresses these questions little by little as she tries to translate a somewhat hazy description of a complaint into a more specific behavioral picture. The following example of this information-gathering process involves an eighth-grade teacher who has arranged a meeting with the school social worker:

Social Worker: You mentioned you had a student you were concerned about and that you wanted us to talk about.

Teacher: Yes, I need to talk with you about Greg, one of the students in my sixth-period class. I'm really worried about him. He seems like a powder keg waiting to go off.

Social Worker: What do you mean exactly?

Teacher: Well, he seems ready to explode about something that I can't put my finger on. He didn't seem to be like this when school first started, but now he seems tight and constrained and keeps to himself. He never gets involved in what we're doing in the class.

Social Worker: How long has this been going on?

Teacher: He's been in this mood for the past several weeks. At first, I just thought he was having a bad day. You know, one of those typical middle schooler ups and downs. But he hasn't come out of it.

Social Worker: What are some of the things you see him doing in class that signal to you he's in this mood? For example, how do you see him acting with you or with other students in the class?

Teacher: With me, he seems detached. Like he's miles away from me and what we're trying to do in class. He's there in his seat, but he doesn't seem to be listening to anything I say.

Social Worker: Almost like he's preoccupied with thinking of something else?

Teacher: That's right. With the other students, he seems to have pulled away too. I don't know if something has happened to him at school or at home or what. I've tried getting him to talk with me a couple different times. But he was just really tight-lipped. He said there was no problem. But to me he seemed really angry. I asked if he were angry at me or at something that might have happened in class or here at school, but he said no.

If the practitioner is not sure what is meant by a certain answer, he should not move on to another topic. Instead, he can say, "I'm not sure I understand what you are saying here," thereby taking on the responsibility for needing further clarification rather than giving the message that the speaker is being too vague. Also, requesting that the speaker give an example is often one of the best ways to get specific behavioral information. Not only does it provide a more detailed picture of how the speaker sees the problem, it may also reveal who else is part of the problem (for example, it may be that two students are engaged in some problematic interaction), as well as make more apparent who else is concerned about the problem behavior (for example, several teachers may be concerned about a particular student).

In addition to getting a report on who is doing what that presents a problem, brief strategic practitioners always want to know to whom is this a problem and why? Although the answers to these two questions may appear self-evident, the practitioner must not assume such an understanding of the problem situation for several reasons. First, answers to these questions allow her to more clearly determine who is most concerned about a particular problem. Second, such questions also allow her to assess how serious the problem is perceived to be by those involved. Finally, such questions allow her to determine whether the problem is one for which she can offer assistance. For example, some students may need assessment and remediation of specific intellectual or physical capacities. Obviously, for such problems a treatment intervention would probably be ill-suited.

To assess to whom the complaint is a problem, each person involved in the interactions around the problem should be asked, How is the situation a problem? For instance, in the case of the eighth-grade boy described above, when the student came in at the teacher's request to meet with the school social worker, the following dialogue ensued.

Social Worker: You were saying that Mrs. Paige [the teacher referring the student] had asked you to meet with me.

Student: Uh-huh.

Social Worker: Could you fill me in as to why you think she wanted you to see me?

Student: Well, I don't know exactly. But I guess, because she's asked me several times if I was mad at her or angry about something, that she wants me to talk with you about that.

Social Worker: And what about you? Do you see this as a problem?

Student: I don't know.

Social Worker: It may be that you don't even think that you've gotten mad when she thinks you have. You might not even see it the way she does.

Student: Well, there have been a couple of times I've been steaming about the way I was pushed around by a guy at my locker before class, but that's just been a couple of times.

Social Worker: And what did you do then?

Student: I don't know. I guess I kept thinking about how I needed to beat up on him. You know, so he'll know he can't push me around.

Social Worker: And is that what happened?

Student: No, the guy keeps skipping school or getting expelled so I haven't been able to get to him.

Social Worker: So, you haven't really had a chance to let him know how angry you are with him by letting him have it.

Student: No, but I guess I'm not worrying about it as much. After all, I haven't even seen the guy in over a week.

Although further inquiry and follow-up will be needed to check this matter out, it appears from this interview that the boy's angry attitude is more of a problem for the teacher than for the student. Thus it may be that one person's idea of the seriousness of a problem is quite different from another's. Inquiries of this kind are important not only in determining the relative seriousness of the complaint to various people, but also in assessing whether the problem is something that can be solved.

In addition to asking what the problem is and clarifying to whom it is a problem, it is also important to determine why individuals have elected to deal with a problem at a particular time. A question such as "What made you decide you needed to do something about this problem at this time?" helps to further clarify the nature of the complaint and often throws a different light on the nature of the problem situation. It may reveal, for example, that the person demonstrating the problem is less concerned about the problem than someone else (a parent or teacher) who has directed him to seek help. In such situations, the handling of the situation differs greatly from circumstances in which the person demonstrating the problem is self-motivated. (If you recall, we discussed this special type of situation in Chapter Four.) It also may be that the problem is much more longstanding than it first appears.

Together with investigating the nature of the complaint, the practitioner always determines what the person with the problem or those persons closely involved with him have been trying to do to resolve the problem (Watzlawick, Weakland, and Fisch, 1974). Because the brief strategic view holds that problems are maintained by the very efforts the problem person and others make to solve the problem, it is essential that the school practitioner get a complete picture of just what those efforts have been—especially those currently being made. This information is crucial, for it is from learning about the specific ways in which people are currently responding to the problem that the counselor will discern the basic thrust of the various efforts to solve the problem.

Consequently, the second step in the information-gathering effort is to inquire what everyone closely involved with the problem has been doing to try to resolve it. This inquiry too should focus on actual behaviors—what people are doing and saying in their attempts to deal with the problem. In the following example, a second-grade teacher is complaining to a school psychologist about one of her students who is distracting other students.

Psychologist: It sounds like Debbie does a number of things to distract other students. When she starts making faces at other students, which you say is one way she gets others distracted, what do you do to try and turn things around?

Teacher: I've done just about everything I can think of.

Psychologist: What have you tried recently?

Teacher: Well, I have consequences for all the students when they talk out of turn or distract others. I warn them once, then put their name on the board, which means they don't earn the right to a free play activity. So with Debbie, I warned her and then put her name on the board.

Psychologist: And what happened then?

Teacher: She just acted like it didn't bother her.

Psychologist: And so how did you respond to that?

Teacher: I kept her in after school.

Psychologist: How did she respond to that?

Teacher: Well, I made her work on her school assignments. And she just itched around in that chair. I never knew how many contortions a little girl could get her body into. She didn't do her work, but I made her sit there the whole forty-five minutes.

Psychologist: Then what did you do?

Teacher: Well, I'd had enough for one day. I let her go home, but I didn't feel I'd won that round at all. She just seems to delight in doing the opposite of what I tell her to do. And I've done just about everything I can think of to break her of that habit.

A tentative picture of how the little girl's misbehavior is being responded to by the teacher can be formed from this account. While further information is necessary to get a fuller view of the entire problem/solution cycle, it appears that "everything" in the teacher's response to this child's behavior consists of variations on the theme of "I demand that you do what I say." Since this theme represents the basic thrust of the teacher's current attempts to solve the problem and it has been unsuccessful, it is essential to avoid it in devising a new approach to the problem.

There are several methods the school practitioner can use to gather information about what people are doing in relation to the problem. Two such methods are tracking the sequence of action and reaction around the problem behavior through specific questions and observing how those involved actually act out these patterns of response and counter-response.

It is often necessary to ask those involved to be clearer in describing their specific responses to the problem behavior. This is particularly necessary when the speaker offers only vague general descriptions or interpretations of the problem behavior and his response to it. To translate a person's vague language into a behavioral account, it is often useful to visualize oneself as a slow-motion camera tracking every feature of an event: Who is on the scene? What specifically happens? Then what happens? The following dialogue illustrates the level of persistence required to extract this type of detailed information.

Counselor: What do you do when John uses bad language in class?

Teacher: I don't know what to do.

Counselor: So what do you do?

Teacher: What can I do?

Counselor: I am not sure what you can do, but what do you do?

Teacher: I've tried everything.

Counselor: What have you tried?

Teacher: Nothing works.

Counselor: When was the last time nothing worked?

Teacher: Yesterday.

Counselor: How did it not work?

Teacher: I just gave up.

Counselor: And how did you give up?

Teacher: I just grabbed John by his collar and told him I would not have any more of it, that I would write a note home to his mother telling her to call me for a conference about this.

Counselor: What happened then?

Teacher: John didn't care at all. He just smiled and played with a pencil in his hand.

Counselor: Then what happened?

Teacher: I proceeded to write the note and told him to take it home.

Counselor: Did he take it home?

Teacher: I don't know if it ever got there, but I called his mother that night anyhow, and she assured me that she would reprimand John and handle the matter at home.

As can be seen, this tracking of the interaction around a problem behavior can be very hard to do for several reasons. First, most people tend to talk in generalities and give highly subjective accounts of their own and others' behavior. In addition, although most parents and teachers welcome efforts to be participants in this information-gathering process, they may be unused to responding to questions asking them to detail their responses to a student. In order not to give them the feeling they are not making themselves understood, the practitioner may need to take a one-down position. For example, the practitioner might choose to convey that her persistent questioning is the result of her own personal limitation in understanding the problem by saying, "I'm afraid I'm just one of these people with a very concrete mind. I hope you won't mind giving me an example of what you mean, so I can picture it." This type of approach can go far toward preserving good will in the face of persistent questioning.

There are often opportunities to see firsthand what people are doing and saying in dealing with the problem behavior. Because these opportunities are often untainted by the perception of the person reporting the events, they represent very useful sources of information about how the problem is being handled. Often such a playing out of the reactions and counter-reactions around problem behavior can be triggered with very little coaching. For example, in the following situation a school counselor is meeting with two fifth-grade students who have been referred for constantly belittling each other in the classroom.

Counselor: Mrs. Greene has asked that I talk with both of you about how you seem to put each other down.

First Student: I'm not putting her down. She just keeps on opening her big fat mouth when she's not supposed to.

Second Student: Is that so? Well, who do you think you are, dummy?

First Student: You're just such a busybody! If you just kept your nose out of my business. . . .

Second Student: You're just mad because Susan spent the night at my house this weekend.

First Student: I wouldn't mind if you two didn't talk about me all night!

It is easy to see what each student is doing and saying here. One does not have to ask for a secondhand account.

Consequently, this mode of observing the problem behavior and the reactions that maintain it provides an efficient means of gathering information about how the problem is being responded to. A key point to keep in mind in using this observational method is that the practitioner must maintain a neutral position concerning the views expressed by the people present until she has planned what to do. Thus, the practitioner needs to listen to how each person perceives the problem, its possible causes, and its solution without offering an opinion regarding the validity of any of these views. Interpretations or advice should be offered only after considering how they will be received.

Most brief strategic practitioners consider that the questions they ask about the outcomes expected from intervention should convey a message about how the intervention will be conducted—that is, that it will focus on changing a specific, observable behavior rather than some inferred internal psychological state or pattern of family relationships (Rosenthal and Bergman, 1986). However, these questions can also help to define the problem more clearly and translate it into observable behavior.

This phase of information gathering is considered the most difficult by many practitioners. It concerns what the person is aiming for in seeking the school practitioner's help (Fisch, Weakland, and Segal, 1982). What would the person consider a significant change to come out of the intervention effort? Because such a change must be defined in behavioral terms, and yet be small enough to make a realistic first step, it is often hard for people to answer this question, for several reasons. First, since most people have a much clearer idea about what they don't want than what they do want, they may have difficulty in defining what they want to see as a result of intervention. Rather than taking this as a sign that they are perverse or unmotivated, the practitioner should keep in mind that lack of clarity on this subject is very typical. Consequently, when the practitioner asks someone, What would you see as a first step indicating that a small but important change has occurred in the problem?, she should expect that that person may need assistance in coming up with a concrete answer.

Sometimes someone will describe a psychological condition she wants to see changed. For example, she may say, "I want him to feel better about himself," or, "I want him to respect me," or, "I want to feel less shy." Since these goals depend on inferences about psychological states, it is necessary to have the client develop a more concrete, behavioral goal, as in the following example.

Student: I'm just so unhappy with how I act. I wish I weren't so shy.

Counselor: What would be one way you would act differently if you weren't so shy?

Student: I wouldn't be such a mouse in class.

Counselor: I'm not sure I understand what you mean by that.

Student: You know, I'd talk up more. I'd answer the teacher's question instead of dreading she might call on me.

Counselor: So one thing you'd like to see come out of our getting together is for you to be able to answer your teacher's question without feeling so worried about how you were doing?

Student: Yeah.

In contrast to the situation above, other clients may have an overabundance of specific intervention goals. In these situations, the person may start off with one concern and then switch to another, and then to another. If the practitioner notices this shifting around, it is important for her to take measures to get a single focus defined. (Obviously, in situations in which more than one person is being worked with, it would be normal for each person to have a somewhat different focus.) One way to handle this kind of situation is for the practitioner to ask the person to define his priorities.

Fisch, Weakland, and Segal (1982, p. 81) report an interesting way to do this in which the practitioner takes a one-down position, assuming responsibility for not knowing which focus to take. For example, she might say, "You really have brought up a number of significant problems. But my capacity to understand things—much less have us figure out what to do about them—is too limited to deal with more than one thing at a time. I just get kind of muddled. So could you tell me what seems to you the major thing right now, the one that is most important to change, if possible?" In the following example, a school counselor used these tactics to assist a teacher in formulating a smaller, more workable goal for her intervention with a first-grade girl.

Counselor: It sounds like there are a lot of things about Sonya that you are worried about.

Teacher: Yes, Sonya just doesn't have any friends or know how to make them. I've tried putting her with other little girls when I team up in workshop activities, but those relationships don't carry over at all onto the playground. Often she just stands by herself while the other little girls play. And I've had to make sure she's team captain so that she's not left the last one to be picked for a team.

Counselor: So learning how to make friends is an area where you think she needs to develop more skills?

Teacher: Part of the problem is that the little girls don't want to play with her because she comes to school so dirty and raggedy looking.

Counselor: So her appearance is a problem?

Teacher: Yes, if I could change her appearance, then maybe that could bring about some changes in the other children toward her. But I don't think her mother really cares. You know what I mean? She just doesn't seem to really bother with how she looks.

Counselor: So you don't think you would get much backing on this from home?

Teacher: No, I think whatever we do for Sonya would have to come from school. I just don't think her mother really cares how she looks. You know, I was thinking that one thing that might work to get other little girls to play with her would be to have her have a toy they would like to play with, too. The other little girls bring their Barbie dolls to school sometimes, but Sonya never has anything to play with. She's always on the outside. You know, I could buy her her own Barbie, and we could keep it at school, and when they have playtime she would have something to share that the other little girls would like, too.

Counselor: So you're thinking that would be a way she could get them to play with her? You know I'm impressed with the amount of thought and effort you've put into trying to help this child. But I'm also overwhelmed with all the different things you see this child needing help with. To help me know where you and I should start, could you tell me what you see as the major thing right now you feel is the most important to change, if possible?

Teacher: Well, that's hard to decide. But I guess her having someone with whom she can play is the most important thing.

Counselor: So if there was someone with whom Sonya seemed to enjoy playing during playtime at school, that would be an important change?

Teacher: Yes.

Other clients may give far too ambitious a goal. In these instances it is important to help the person formulate smaller, more realistic steps. Sometimes, by asking for clarification, the practitioner can help translate somewhat grandiose expectations into more realistic ones. By acting confused and slow, the practitioner can also create opportunities for greater clarification in this area.

To summarize, there are several types of information that must be gathered to plan one's interventions effectively.

Often the practitioner will feel pressured to act quickly to solve a problem. However, if he fails to take the time to get adequate information about the problem, how it is being and has been handled, and what people want as a change, he runs the risk of not knowing what to avoid in attempting to solve the problem. Therefore, even though the practitioner may feel he is taking a great deal of time gathering information, he must remember that an intervention cannot be effectively planned without it. Furthermore, such information gathering can also be a channel for building a relationship with the people involved. The practitioner can empathize with how it appears a person is feeling in dealing with the situation and underscore the positive intent of her efforts to deal with the problem despite her lack of success.

Besides knowing what people are doing in response to a particular problem, the practitioner must ascertain what personal beliefs are dictating how people respond to one another and to the problem behavior. Not only are these personal beliefs important keys to understanding why people choose certain patterns of response and not others, they are also the channel through which the practitioner can motivate people to follow a new way of responding to the problem. Regrettably, this type of information is not right at people's fingertips. It must be inferred from the language people use and the positions they take about the problem, its cause, and its solution. For this reason, finding out about someone's beliefs requires a different mode of information gathering. In the next chapter we describe the nature of this process and its use in planning an intervention.

CHAPTER 6

Assessing and Making Use of Client Beliefs

Often, the particular beliefs people hold as to why a problem exists and how it should be responded to are factors that prevent them from resolving it. These same beliefs, however, can be used to motivate people to respond differently and more effectively to problems. To increase people's motivation, the practitioner needs to know which beliefs to assess and how to use them to increase people's cooperation. In this chapter, the focus will be on how to assess and use key beliefs to change people's response to a problem.

Someone attempting to resolve a persistent student problem will have definite beliefs about why the problem exists and what should be done about it. These beliefs are the reason why certain ways of responding are followed while others are ignored. Unfortunately, these beliefs cannot be discovered by direct questioning. Instead, they must be deduced from what the person says and how she reports the situation. Consider the following account a high school teacher gave a school counselor concerning a tenth-grade student who constantly disrupted his class: "Tim's one of those kinds of kids who can really get your goat. He's much more interested in proving he's top dog than learning anything in my class. He constantly baits me into coming down hard on him and then sees if he can get out from under it. His latest trick is to get others distracted and then, when I catch him, deny that he's doing anything wrong and say that it's the other kid's fault. Of

94

course that always starts another argument as the other fellow tries to defend himself. Then they're off fighting again, and it's total chaos. I have to be right there constantly keeping my thumb on him like some kind of jail warden to keep him from totally disrupting the class. He's just a real pain in the neck to have in class."

What beliefs about the student and the nature of the problem situation underlie this teacher's report? The teacher's comments suggest that he regards this student as aggravating, difficult to control, and essentially bad. Consequently, the teacher is irritated by the student. Not only do his beliefs about the nature of the problem trigger certain emotional responses in the teacher, they also trigger certain ideas as to how the problem should be solved. For this teacher, the solution should be firm control, that is, keeping his thumb on the student. Thus, beliefs concerning how and why the student is misbehaving and how the student should be responded to keep the teacher committed to a certain course of action. Even when the student's behavior does not improve, the teacher may continue to follow this course of action because he believes it is the only appropriate way to handle the situation.

Assessing such beliefs is crucial to deciding how to intervene, for two reasons. First, identifying the kinds of beliefs a person holds helps clarify the major thrust of his solution efforts. Second, the justification that the practitioner gives someone for engaging in a particular solution shift must reflect that person's key beliefs to have a motivational impact. For example, in the case above, the teacher's description of the student suggested that he saw the student as the problem and himself as victimized by the student. Given this set of beliefs, his response was to correct the student, largely by demanding that the student follow his rules. However, further inquiry revealed that in this particular situation the teacher's response triggered more acting out from the student rather than less, which in turn led to even more control behavior from the teacher.

One way to interrupt this circular process of acting out

and controlling would be to have the teacher reverse his position. Instead of demanding that he be obeyed, the teacher could take a one-down position with respect to the student. Instead of stern threats and punishment, the teacher would acknowledge that he could not make the student want to be there, that the student's acting out was obviously a signal that he did not wish to be in the class, and that it was all right with the teacher if he left the class.

Given the teacher's current position relative to the boy, this kind of shift in his response to the student would have little chance of being considered unless the shift was presented in terms of the teacher's beliefs. Consequently, although the counselor might recognize the provocative effect the teacher's behavior actually had on the student, she would not tell the teacher this, since such a statement would only antagonize him and reduce his cooperation. Instead, she would agree with the teacher's beliefs by saying, "He must realize that as his teacher you have a right to expect him to be appropriately respectful of you." Only after signaling agreement with the teacher's beliefs would the counselor propose a shift to a new solution behavior. However, even this would be presented as a way of being in an authoritative position. For example, the counselor might explain that it appeared the student rarely paid attention to what the teacher told him in class. The counselor might then suggest that this occurred because the teacher was so predictable that the student simply tuned him out. If the teacher wanted to get through to him and let him know who was really in charge, he would first need to get his attention. One way he could do this was by becoming unpredictable. Certain one-down behaviors could then be framed as illustrations of this approach.

As can be seen from this example, beliefs are considered neither good nor bad, correct nor incorrect in brief strategic intervention. Rather, beliefs are used to facilitate cooperation and aid in resolving an ongoing problem. To employ them effectively, it is important that the practitioner first assess the kinds of beliefs under which people are operating.

One set of beliefs especially relevant to designing effective interventions are those a client holds about the nature of the problem and its presumed cause. These beliefs are often expressed as people describe the problem and its history, as the following reports show.

The first case involves a student who believes that the problem is with her teacher: "I just hate my math teacher. She's always on my case, criticizing what I do and putting me down in front of the other kids. You know what she did to me yesterday? First she told me how sloppy my paper was, then she told me I even think like a slob! I couldn't take it anymore. I walked out of her class. You know what she did then? She wrote me up for leaving class without permission, and now I have to serve three days' detention after school. I just can't stand her!"

In the second case, the teacher believes that the student needs her help: "I am so concerned about Sonya. She is such a little loner. She roams around the room by herself all the time. None of the other little girls want to play with her. I've tried many times setting up activities where she can be in a leader role—like making her captain and being the one to pick others for a team, or having her work with just one other little girl on a workshop activity. But nothing seems to work. She just doesn't seem to have any friends or know how to make them."

As can be seen here, the beliefs held about the nature of the problem are presented as the facts of the case. These beliefs fall into a predictable set of categories. People either define themselves as having the problem, or define it as concerning someone else. If they define someone else as the problem, they present themselves as either victimized by a person who is bad (as in the first case) or concerned about a person who is troubled (as in the second case). If a person defines himself as the problem, he presents himself as either struggling with a problem that is controllable or troubled by a problem over which voluntary control is not possible. In addition, a person will usually convey beliefs about the possibility and urgency of a problem's resolution. Either he will take the position that the problem is a painful one for which change is pressingly needed, or he will report his condition as undesirable but not particularly uncomfortable or in need of urgent change. An example of the first position is provided by a teacher having difficulty controlling her class: "I know I need to work on being more in control of my class. I have such a hard time getting them to settle down and listen to my instructions. It's a constant battle just getting them to sit still long enough to finish telling them what they're to do. I've tried laying down rules and consequences with them, but somehow things always come unraveled. I've even taken two of them who are the hardest to control outside and talked to them about what I expect. But that helped for only a little while, and now they're back to being rambunctious. Even the good kids are beginning to act up."

An example of the second position is provided by a student who dislikes going to school: "I know it's important that I come to school. My mom and everybody else keep telling me that it's important, but this school is such a drag. The teachers don't really care if I'm here or not, and the students are just stuck up. I know that you want to help me, and I want to get going in something, but I just don't think this school is for me. I know I need to figure out something if I'm not going to go here, but I'm not sure when I'll be ready to do that. How about if I come in when I decide what I need to do?"

This second position is often taken by a person who is pressured by someone else to get help for his problem. As these two examples demonstrate, people often define both how urgent they consider the problem and how difficult they believe its resolution will be. Such beliefs can range from perceiving the problem as almost unsolvable to perceiving it as difficult but solvable. Furthermore, people also signal whether they believe the problem requires immediate attention or not.

Because these beliefs are usually presented as the facts of the situation, it is easy for the practitioner not to see them as beliefs, particularly when her own beliefs about the problem closely parallel those of the person involved. In those instances where one is uncertain as to the nature of these beliefs, asking "Why do you think this problem exists?" or "Why has this problem developed the way it has?" can help clarify matters.

After the practitioner determines which of the above-mentioned beliefs are operating, how does she make use of this information? First, these beliefs can be used to clarify the underlying thrust of current solution efforts. Second, they can be used to motivate the people involved to comply with a proposed change in their response to the problem.

The client's beliefs as to who has the problem and how much voluntary control exists over it usually shape the basic thrust of that person's attempts to solve the problem. As Table 2 shows, individuals who report feeling victimized either by themselves (type one) or someone else (type three) typically feel angry and resentful about the problem and respond by attempting to master it through coercion. By contrast, individuals who believe their problem is beyond conscious control (types two and four) often present themselves as worried or benevolently concerned about a troubling personal condition or problem person. Because they believe the problem is awful and cannot be changed through voluntary effort, they may bend all efforts to avoiding the situation. However, such individuals may continue to wish a different performance were possible. This inherently contradictory message is typically met by a counter-response carrying a similar message. In type four situations, for example, it may be characterized by the statements "I'm not really telling you what I want you to do" and "OK, I'm not really refusing either."

Since people often consider their efforts to resolve a problem the only sane thing to do, simply telling someone to stop what he has been doing and do the opposite will usually be resisted strongly. Thus, once the practitioner decides what would be the best way to respond differently to the problem situation, she must figure out a way to justify this new response so that it is consistent with the person's current beliefs. This is done by redefining the task so that it fits with the person's current beliefs.

Table 2. Problem-Maintaining Responses Triggered by Certain Beliefs
About the Problem Situation.

Beliefs About Locus of the Problem

Beliefs About Control of Problem	Person Believes He Is the Problem	Person Believes Another Person Is the Problem
Believes Problem Is Under Voluntary Control	Type One. Because problem behavior is believed to be under voluntary control of the person reporting the problem, efforts to resolve it consist of forcing oneself to behave less problematically in dealing with involuntary behavior.	Type Three. Because problem behavior is believed to involve another person who is believed to consciously choose not to respond in the way preferred by the complaining party, efforts to resolve the problem consist of demanding a response from the other.
Believes Problem Is Not Under Voluntary Control	Type Two. Because problem behavior is believed to be something over which the complaining person has no conscious control, efforts to solve the problem consist of avoiding something that is greatly dreaded or feared.	Type Four. Because problem behavior is believed to involve another person who cannot help himself, efforts to resolve the problem consist of avoiding making a direct request concerning the behavior, yet still hoping it will be resolved on its own.

To do this effectively, it is necessary for the practitioner to accommodate the beliefs of the person she is trying to motivate to act differently. She must first carefully assess the nature of the person's beliefs and then use them to justify a specific change in action. As an example, consider a case in which a school psychologist gets information about a fourth-grade student from both the girl's teacher and her mother. The teacher tells him: "Kim's problem is that she's used to being able to get her way. Now that her classmates are older, they just won't put up with her bossing them around. They avoid her because of her bossiness. As a result, she now baits them into paying attention to her by constantly teasing them and starting fights. She's just going to have to realize that she can't have her way all the time, that there are other people in the world besides her." The mother tells him: "I'm really worried about Kim. She's had trouble fitting in with the other students in her class from the very first. She just doesn't seem to know how to make friends. Lately she's really been wearing her heart on her sleeve a lot, getting into fights a number of times with the other kids. I know she's just very hurt that they haven't included her in things. I really believe if she could just find a way to feel better about herself, it might be easier for the other kids to accept her."

These two adults have distinctly different views about the same student. The teacher regards the student as uncaring of others, selfish, and essentially bad. Consequently, she seems irritated with her. In contrast, the mother takes a more sympathetic view. She sees the girl's fighting behavior as a sign of her underlying unhappiness in not fitting in. She is not bad, she is troubled. These differing perceptions of the nature of the student's problem trigger different emotional responses and different ideas as to how the problem should be solved. Now, if the school psychologist were to suggest that the teacher try to be more understanding of Kim's situation, he would be likely to meet with resistance from this particular teacher because this explanation does not mesh with the teacher's view of the girl. Similarly, if the psychologist were to suggest that the mother punish the girl when she engages in bullying or fighting, he would risk making the mother resistant to his ideas since this recommendation runs counter to the mother's beliefs. What is indicated here is for the school psychologist to treat the mother and the teacher as separate clients, each needing a distinctive rationale to induce her to try what may very well be the same behavior. For example, whatever the school psychologist directs the teacher to do would need to be framed as helping to establish appropriate control. In contrast, any actions the mother would be instructed to take would be presented as therapeutic for the child.

In summary, tailoring recommendations for changed behavior to the unique beliefs the client holds as to the nature of the problem and its solution is useful for two reasons. First, it helps to avoid triggering people to resist certain suggestions. Second, it maximizes their compliance with the practitioner's suggestions because it uses their current beliefs to justify responding differently. In the next chapter the process for considering what to recommend in terms of changed behavior will be described.

CHAPTER 7

Planning and Implementing an Intervention

To resolve a persistent student problem rapidly, it is important that the practitioner carefully plan how to direct those involved to act differently in responding to the problem. Unlike intervention approaches in which a practitioner waits for the client to make a move and then responds, in this approach precise pre-session planning is required. Not only must the practitioner determine what might be the most strategic shift in the current solution efforts, she must also devise specific steps for implementing this shift and present them with an explanation that makes them more palatable to those involved. She must then monitor this change effort over time. In this chapter, each of these aspects of intervention planning will be described.

As a first step toward eliminating problem-maintaining behaviors, the practitioner needs to decide who is involved in the problem and how they are involved. In those situations where it is the problem-bearer alone who misapplies a solution, the practitioner's sole task is to block that person's solution. Often, however, problems are maintained by the well-intentioned efforts of others (for example, teachers, school

Note: Portions of this chapter are excerpted from Amatea, E., and Sherrard, P. A. "Reversing the School's Response: A New Approach to Resolving Persistent School Problems." *American Journal of Family Therapy*, 1989, *17*, 15–26. Reprinted here by permission of Brunner/Mazel, Inc.

counselors, other students, or parents), and the practitioner must thus be concerned with blocking their solutions as well. For example, in the case of Niki, the little girl who vomited at school and at home, the problem was maintained both by what Niki was doing and by what concerned adults at school and at home were doing. The adults' efforts to get Niki to try harder not to vomit were not effective. However, getting these adults to stop their efforts was not sufficient; another response was needed. In this case, a two-pronged intervention strategy was necessary. One prong centered on helping Niki supplant her original response of trying to make herself not vomit, and the second focused on blocking the school staff from giving Niki the message that she should try harder. Consequently, deciding whether to intervene at the individual or interpersonal level depends on the practitioner's assessment of what is maintaining the problem behavior. It may be that the practitioner needs to target his interventions at more than one level.

There may also be two or more vicious-circle problems nested together. Rather than just targeting one, the practitioner may decide to intervene in all of them. One example of this approach involved a third-grade boy named George who constantly failed to complete his school assignments. The boy's parents had been asked by his teacher and the school counselor to see that he finished all incomplete class assignments at home. They were given a feedback checksheet to record which assignments had been completed. Nonetheless, the boy continued to neglect his classwork; he would daydream, dawdle at his work, and only do what he wished. Furthermore, his mother reported she often allowed her son to escape from finishing his assignments at home, and she seemed resentful about pressuring him to complete his work. The school now saw the problem not only as George but as the parents falling down on their responsibilities. The parents admitted to the counselor that they dreaded each phone contact from the school.

Since the homework checksheet had not resulted in any improvement in the boy's situation, the counselor decided to employ a different approach. First, she met with the boy's teacher to gather detailed information about how the teacher responded to the boy's lack of follow-through on assignments. The teacher seemed to view the boy benevolently—seeing him as being discouraged rather than bad when she gave him an assignment. She was overly patient with him, giving him many reminders and much special attention. When the counselor met with the boy's mother, she discovered a similar response. Both teacher and mother believed they should not directly command George to complete his work. By contrast, George's stepfather of two years appeared to have no problem commanding George to work, and George did not seem to resent the stepfather's directives. The stepfather insisted that the teacher needed to be much firmer rather than expect that of George's mother.

The counselor planned a series of interventions that shifted the response of key people at school to George; at the same time, she asked his mother and stepfather not to change. First, she met with George's teacher and persuaded the teacher to be more direct in her requests of George. By reporting that she had discovered that George interpreted the teacher's efforts as indicating she thought he was dumb and could not do the work, and suggesting that giving a clear, direct message to George would let him know she knew he was smart enough to do the work, the counselor attempted to change the teacher's interpretation of George's disinterest in classwork. The counselor then coached the teacher to give more direct instructions to George in three areas: He was told to stay on-task in his classwork, to not talk out, and to stay in his seat. Further, the teacher was coached to explain to George that she had just spent time in a fourth-grade class and realized that he would not be ready to move into fourth grade if he did not start doing these three things. Since she knew he wanted to move on with his class, she was going to see if he could demonstrate that he was ready to move on. If he failed to make these changes, it would mean he really was not old enough and would need to stay in third grade another year.

The counselor then met with George's parents and acknowledged that the earlier plan of having them force George to complete his classwork at home had been a total failure and that they were right in saying that the problem was that George's teacher was not firm enough. Because there was a strong possibility that George would not pass to fourth grade due to his current performance, the counselor reported that the teacher had decided to specify exactly what George was to do to be ready for fourth grade. The counselor then outlined the specific changes the teacher was instituting. In addition, the counselor reaffirmed that while she knew George's parents would want to know what George's teacher was doing, they were not in any way to try to help her with it. After all, the school was the party that needed to let George know what he had to do. The counselor and parents talked about the fact that though George would probably have some difficulty shifting over, he seemed to be a flexible little boy and would probably change.

As the teacher became clearer in her requests, George became more openly resistant. He complained to his parents that the teacher was mean and gave him too much homework, and he got sullen and pouty in school. His teacher was somewhat surprised by his change in attitude, but (with support from the counselor) was able to sustain her demands. After two weeks of experiencing the consequences of being off-task (for example, being sent to the principal's office), George began to stay in his seat and not talk out, and over the next two months he completed enough of his work to be promoted to fourth grade.

This example illustrates how a combination of interventions was designed to provoke a change in the way the boy responded to the teacher, the parents responded to the school, and the boy responded to his parents. Rather than demand the parents' cooperation, the school cooperated with the parents by assuming the responsibility for solving the problem. The parents could then stop defending themselves and their lack of success in getting George to complete his assignments and allow their son to take responsibility for his own behavior.

In both of the cases described above a particular approach to intervention planning is illustrated. First, the key elements and people in the interaction around the problem are identified. An important clue for the school mental health professional trying to determine who to include in this interactional assessment is provided by Lindquist, Molnar, and Brauchman (1987), who characterize a school-related problem as a problem at school that disturbs the family, a problem in the family that disturbs the school, or a problem at school that does not disturb the family. These characterizations suggest which people (for example, those at school, those at home, or those both at school and at home) to include in the intervention effort.

Next, the various actions taken by these people in addressing the problem are reviewed so that the practitioner will know what does not work and can determine if the situation warrants a brief strategic intervention. If such an intervention is warranted, a careful assessment is then made of how the problem organizes the interaction around it, with particular attention to the sequence of behaviors and their meaning to each participant. From this information judgments are then made concerning the basic thrust of these solution efforts, how open the persons involved are to the practitioner's influence, and to what extent the problem behavior is defined as under voluntary control. Specific solution shifts are then formulated, and action steps are identified by which these solution shifts can be implemented. Then a rationale for these actions is developed to motivate those involved to follow the prescribed steps. Finally, the action directives and rationale are delivered, and steps are taken to monitor and sustain these new ways of responding. These steps and the particular questions associated with them are shown in Exhibit 1. Let us look at each of these steps in more detail.

To determine whether actions in response to a student's problem behavior are inadvertently provoking or maintaining it, the practitioner needs to collect detailed information about the specifics of the problem situation and how it is being

Exhibit 1. Overall Process of Planning
a Brief Strategic Intervention.

Step One: Gather Information About the Nature of the Problem and Decide Whether Brief Strategic Intervention Is Warranted. What does the problem look like? What is being said or done by whom to whom? When, where, and how? Ask for action and dialogue. Who else is affected by the problem and how? What does the problem make people do or not do? Why is help being sought at this particular time? Are there particular concrete deficits or traumatic events that are triggering the problem behavior (for example, academic deficiencies, loss through death or divorce, or chaotic family context)?

Step Two: Establish Who Is Most Affected by the Problem. Who is defined as the person needing help? Who is affected by the problem and how? Is the person reporting the problem defined as the one needing help? If not, who is involved? Are these people in conflict with one another? Who is most upset about the problem?

Step Three: Find Out How Committed to the Change Effort Is the Person Needing Help. (If the person reporting the problem is committed to seeking change, move on to Step Four.) If the person needing help is not committed to the change effort, use soft-sell tactics such as renegotiating a new complaint. If that does not work, consider working with the person pressuring the problem-bearer to seek help. If that does not work consider using hard-sell tactics such as undermining the person's position.)

Step Four: Gather Information About the Solutions Attempted. What has been done in response to the problem by each person involved with it? Ask for action and dialogue. Be sure to determine if simple, straightforward solutions have been tried, such as direct requests for changed behavior. If the description is quite vague, ask questions such as, What specifically was said or done in response to a particular occurrence of the problem? If the person acts helpless, acknowledge the difficulty of his position and direct him to carry out his usual response and report back on this process.

Step Five: Analyze the Client's Beliefs. Determine what is important to the client and what makes sense to her. For example, what is the client's best guess as to why the problem has developed and why past efforts to resolve it have failed?

Step Six: Determine What Would Be Considered a Small but Significant Outcome of the Intervention. What might be the first sign that the person is on his way to getting better? If the outcome is stated in specific terms and is consistent with the presenting problem, move on to the next step. If the outcome is too vague and general, or too large a step to be realistic, ask the person to specify one small sign of improvement.

**Exhibit 1. Overall Process of Planning
a Brief Strategic Intervention, Cont'd.**

Step Seven: Identify the Underlying Solution Thrust. What is the common thread underlying the various efforts to resolve the problem? Does the client view the problem-bearer as bad and respond with coercive tactics? Or does the client view the problem-bearer as troubled by conditions beyond his control and avoid taking direct action?

Step Eight: Formulate the Most Strategic Shift in the Current Solution Effort. What response would be the greatest departure from the current ways of responding to the problem?

Step Nine: Develop Specific Action Directives and a Rationale. What specific behaviors could be performed easily and frequently and would epitomize this solution shift? What explanation could be given that would make these actions palatable to the people involved?

Step Ten: Monitor and Sustain the Change Effort. What obstacles might get in the way of following through on the change directives? How might such difficulties be predicted? How will you know if the change effort is working?

handled. To do this, the practitioner obtains a behavioral account of specific instances of the problem behavior and people's response to it (who did what to whom and when) rather than just a general description of the problem situation ("I get upset just thinking about food") or an inferred explanation of the problem behavior ("I just don't feel like going to school"). To develop such a behavioral account, the practitioner needs to solicit a play-by-play account of current instances in which the problem behavior occurs not just from the student demonstrating the problem but from others involved with him. Specific questions (Where and when does the problem occur? How often or how much does it occur? In response to what? To whom is it a problem, and how is it a problem? What is being done to solve the problem and by whom?) help to determine not only the extent of the problem and the people involved, but the basic thrust of the various efforts being made to solve the problem.

As the practitioner accumulates specific information about the student's problem and how it is being addressed, he learns what is not working and must decide whether a brief strategic intervention is warranted. Typically, this approach is considered only when more simple, straightforward methods of changing problematic student behavior (such as direct requests) have failed. To determine whether brief strategic tactics or more intensive therapeutic approaches are appropriate, the practitioner must first determine if one of the following three conditions is operating. First, is the student in such emotional turmoil as the result of a current trauma (for example, a recent divorce, death, or family move) that he cannot act upon direct requests for changed behavior? If this is the case, interventions that restore a sense of control, stability, and nurturance are more appropriate than brief strategic tactics. Second, is a student's life context so disorganized by chronic stressors (for example, an alcoholic parent) as to make it impossible for her to act in a predictable way? If this is the case, intensive individual or family-oriented psychotherapy is more appropriate than brief strategic intervention. Third, are actual deficits in the student's learning abilities causing educational underachievement or emotional difficulties? Except for these three circumstances, brief strategic intervention should be considered when student behavior seems resistant to more direct tactics.

The behavioral account gathered in Step One of Exhibit 1 must be carefully reviewed to discern specific sequences of behavior and the role each participant plays in supporting the problem. Gaps in the sequence are filled in, and information about the meaning of each action to each participant is gathered. Questions such as "What is your best guess as to why this problem has developed?" or "What do you hope will be accomplished by your responding in this way?" may help clarify the meanings of the actions taken to those involved. Once the underlying pattern that connects the various responses becomes clear, alternative ways of responding to the problem can be considered.

As the practitioner reflects upon the basic solution thrust (that is, the pattern connecting the various efforts of those involved to solve the problem) he can imagine what would happen if each participant did something differently and how it would alter the pattern. Clues for deciding which kind of solution shift to apply can be gleaned from determining how the problem is perceived by the people involved. If they appear angry and frustrated and talk as if they feel victimized, they may have been engaged in fighting with themselves or someone else to resolve the problem. Shifting their efforts from fighting to submitting (as in the case of Niki) can have a profound impact. In contrast, some individuals report being worried or fearful about a problem and avoid taking action because they view it as something beyond their personal control. In such instances, shifting their efforts from avoidance to direct effort (as in the case of George) can effectively reverse the problem/solution cycle.

To construct a solution shift, it often helps to consider what specific behaviors might be incompatible with a person's current solution efforts. That is, what actions could a person take that would be the biggest departure from her previous way of responding to the problem? Next, it is important to consider which of those old responses are most central to maintenance of the problem. Finally, the practitioner must determine whether the new responses can be performed frequently enough to have an impact.

After a particular solution shift is selected, the practitioner needs to specify concrete action steps that the school staff and/or the student will take to implement this shift. To do this, the practitioner must think in transactional terms about how to change what people say and do in trying to resolve the problem and be specific in directing participants to act differently. In the case of Niki, for example, simply telling her to stop worrying about vomiting would have had little effect in interrupting her efforts to control her problem vomiting. What was needed was a set of competing responses that could be performed in place of the original behaviors. These responses implement the goal of reversing the predictable sequence that supports the problem and creating a new situation that elicits a new set of responses.

Because a solution shift is often a radical departure from the way those involved with a problem have responded before, it is always necessary to build their motivation to implement the change. To persuade people to try out a new response, the practitioner must provide a rationale that makes it more palatable. Beliefs about the problem can be used to develop an explanation that reframes the meaning associated with the actions suggested. For example, in the case of George, the boy who failed to complete his classwork, an explanation was provided to the teacher that made her continued accommodation of George's behavior less acceptable to her. Moreover, the explanations given George and his parents were somewhat different from those given George's teacher because each explanation is tailored to match the individual's response to and beliefs about the problem.

After participants are provided with both directions and a rationale for acting differently, the practitioner needs to observe the subsequent transactions carefully to see what happens. The steps above are repeated until there is evidence of change in desirable directions. Often it takes a while for the effect of a solution shift to be realized and for reorganization of the behavior around the problem to occur. As evidence of change is noticed, it often helps to test and confirm that change. The practitioner may ask selected individuals to pretend the problem still exists and then observe their response. Or the practitioner may express surprise at what has happened and invite explanations from the participants. In each case, the people involved have an opportunity to affirm the changes they have experienced.

As noted above, understanding the basic thrust of the various efforts being made to solve a problem is crucial to deciding how to get those involved to act differently. This basic solution thrust, according to Fisch, Weakland, and Segal (1982), is discovered by compiling as precise and complete a picture as possible of the nature of the problem and all the specific solution behaviors currently being applied to resolve it. Interestingly, the nature of this basic solution thrust is frequently one of two possibilities: coercion or avoidance (see Table 3). The coercive response typically triggers a counter-response of rejection by the other side, which then triggers a repetition of the coercive effort. This results in a vicious circle in that the more one side pushes to get control, the more the other side responds by rejecting this control. This cycle of coercion and rejection is regularly demonstrated in situations in which a person tries to force a performance from herself that can only occur spontaneously, as well as in situations where one person seeks to command a certain performance from another either by "seeking accord through opposition" or by "attempting to defend oneself through denial" (Fisch, Weakland, and Segal, 1982, p. 113).

The avoidance solution thrust is routinely illustrated when a person attempts to respond to a problem that he perceives as not under his voluntary control. In such situations the problem person usually describes himself (or is described by others) as, on the one hand, unable to help the way he behaves, and, on the other hand, wishing to change the involuntary behavior. Thus one portion of the response is to avoid confronting the problem directly while the other portion is to continue wishing for a changed response. If such a pattern involves another person, one typically finds that the other person responds in a similarly contradictory manner by avoiding acknowledging the request while acting responsive, that is, by refusing the request indirectly. Usually people make statements like "It is not that he will not help himself, but that he cannot" or "It is not that she refuses to change her behavior, it is merely that she is unable to do so." As can be seen in Table 3, this misapplied avoidance thrust results in a circular process of avoidance and counter-avoidance in those situations where an individual seeks either to master a situation by postponement or to get voluntary compliance from another.

How does one determine whether the problematic response is one of coercion or avoidance? Although a person may mention a number of different things he has done to resolve a problem, they are likely to be variations on one of these two solution thrusts. For example, a teacher complaining about a student may say, "I've tried everything I can think of to get her to settle down and quit distracting others. I've

Table 3. Common Coercive and Avoidance Solution Thrusts.

Characteristics of Problem/Solution Cycle	Nature of Current Solution Thrust	Beliefs Underlying Current Thrust
	Coercive Solution Thrusts	
Attempting to coerce spontaneous mental/physical performance from oneself.	Person tries harder to make himself respond in a certain way by means of willpower. Outsiders signal that trying harder will work.	Person believes that his functioning can be willed to happen (is under voluntary control); that trying harder is the only logical route; that not doing anything will only make matters worse. Others view person with benevolence or mixture of exasperation and benevolence.
Attempting to coerce a particular response from another that can only occur voluntarily (for example, to be more loving, respectful, responsive).	Person tries harder to make the other person see the correctness of her request through methods such as demands, harangues, and nagging.	Person believes that because what she wants is only right, just, fair or necessary, the other should do what she commands; that pushing to be treated one-up by the other is the only route; that not doing anything means being taken advantage of; that other is bad or stubborn.
Denying accusations made by another and defending oneself in such a way as to confirm the accuser's suspicions.	Person tries hard to convince another person of his innocence. Person goes to great lengths to defend himself, triggers more suspicions and accusations, and thus more defending.	Person believes that if he tries hard enough he can convince the other of his innocence or competence; that the accuser is unreasonable, unkind, or mistaken; that defending himself is the only sane course of action; that to do nothing would be catastrophic.

	Avoidance Solution Thrusts	
Attempting to master a feared event by postponement.	Person fears he is not ready to master event; thus postpones it to prepare to face it; thus never has an opportunity to learn to master it.	Person believes that best and only way to handle fear is to postpone dealing with what prompts it; that this fear cannot be controlled; that others do not understand the true nature or scope of fear; that others see him as fragile.
Attempting to get someone to do something one wants by having him do it voluntarily.	Person tries to make another comply with her requests by indirectly suggesting the other person comply.	Person believes that it is wrong to directly command the other person's compliance (for example, that the other person must truly want to do it on his own, or that the other person is not able to speak for himself).

Source: Adapted from Fisch, Weakland, and Segal, 1982.

given her warnings; I've sat her away from everyone else; I've taken away her free playtime; I've even made her stay after school." In this situation, "everything" consists of variations on the one central theme of coercing a proper performance from the student. In another case, a child afraid of speaking up in class describes her efforts to deal with her problem in the following way: "I've tried hard to get myself to speak up in class. First, I tried raising my hand and having the teacher call on me, but I'd forget what I was going to say. Then, when that didn't work, I tried getting myself to answer a simple question. But none of these things seemed to work." These measures are both variations on the central thrust of coercing herself to speak up.

As a rule of thumb, if a problem situation is defined by the person involved as voluntary, the person often assumes she should have control over it. Consequently, the typical solution thrust is to seek to coerce the desired performance— even if it is not in fact under voluntary control. In contrast, when the problem behavior is viewed as not under voluntary control, avoidance more often characterizes the nature of the attempted solution thrust. For example, when a youngster fears attending a class where he must make a speech, considers his situation outside his control, and responds by avoiding the situation while at the same time continuing to expect that he should master it, the basic solution thrust is avoidance. Obviously, this solution of avoiding a performance intensifies rather than resolves the student's difficulty with public speaking.

Determining the nature of the current solution thrust allows the practitioner to plan what might be the most strategic shift in it. Only by supplanting the current solution behaviors with quite different ones can the practitioner trigger a strategic shift in the problem behavior. But how does he decide in what direction to shift such solution responses? To have a maximum effect on the problem behavior, brief strategic practitioners regularly advise choosing solution behaviors that differ radically from those currently being applied: "Effective strategies are likely to be ones opposite from the patient's basic thrust" (Fisch, Weakland, and Segal, 1982, p. 115). As Table 4 shows, in the case of coercion, the opposite solution would be to abdicate control. This amounts to a radical shift from trying to be one-up to choosing to be one-down. For example, in a situation in which the teacher was trying to force a student to follow her demands, and the student was resisting those demands, the opposite response to forcing control on the student (that is, trying to get one-up on the student) would be to accept the student's control (that is, acting one-down with respect to the student).

In the case of an avoidance effort, two messages are expressed that inherently contradict each other—postponing action while still holding oneself responsible for a correct performance. To interrupt this particular problem/solution cycle, one can shift to having the person take action rather than avoid it, but with the goal of having an *imperfect* performance. An example of a situation where such a solution shift was needed involved a tenth-grade girl who reported severe anxiety in speaking before her class. In answering the counselor's questions regarding how she had attempted to handle this problem she stated, "Well, I always spend a lot of time trying to choose something I think I can talk about, and I've even read over some ideas about what I should do to make a good speech. But then I started thinking about what usually happens when I'm speaking. I usually get so scared that I totally forget what I am going to say, or my voice and my hands shake so that I can hardly get a word out. I try to put this out of my mind, but I know what is going to happen. Sure enough, when I go to give a speech I get tenser and tenser, even though I try hard not to be. My voice gets shaky, and I can barely think what I'm doing, much less say something. I just try to endure it, but it's awful. I vow I'm never going to get myself into this spot again. It's the worst thing I've ever experienced."

Analyzing this information to identify the girl's current solution thrust, one sees that she perceives her tension as something she has no control over. All of her solution efforts are designed to avoid the feared experience of being noticeably

Table 4. Strategic Shifts in Coercive and Avoidance Solution Efforts.

Characteristics of the Problem/Solution Cycle	Nature of Proposed Solution Shift	Intended Impact	Rationale Presented
Trying to coerce a spontaneous performance from oneself.	Having the person try harder to fail in his performance.	Creating a no-contest structure that interrupts the original effort.	Either explain that it is important to bring on the problem behavior for diagnostic purposes or explain that it is the first step to eventual control.
Coercing a particular response from another that can only occur voluntarily.	To interrupt the response of one-up demandingness, vague requests, or over-statement of one's power by directing person to take one-down position, making requests in casual and nonauthoritarian manner.	To give the other person nothing to fight against.	Agree person is correct but that he has become too predictable and thus is losing the battle.
Denying another's accusations by defending oneself.	Direct defender to agree with the accusations but for reasons hard for accuser to agree with; or confuse the accuser by deciding when and when not to perform behavior.	Create a no-contest situation and confuse accuser.	Can end the game if can make the accuser see how mistaken he is; can do this by agreeing with accusations.

| Attempting to master a feared event by postponement. | Direct person to expose himself to feared task but under conditions of nonmastery, and restrain person from trying to improve. | To provide a worse alternative that the person will defy. | Need to become more appreciative of real dangers involved. To do this must get back in the situation and bring these on only to accept them, not to improve. |
| Attempting to gain compliance thru voluntarism. | Directing person who suggests compliance indirectly to make requests direct even if they are arbitrary. | To make the avoidance of a direct request worse than the direct request. | Describe the indirect stance as harmful and the direct stance as beneficial. |

Source: Adapted from Fisch, Weakland, and Segal, 1982.

nervous in front of an audience. She does this both by attempting to conceal her tension when speaking and by avoiding
opportunities to speak. However, these very behaviors keep
the problem going. The more she thinks about making herself master the situation, the tenser she becomes. To reverse
this general thrust of avoiding a feared event because it is not
mastered, the girl will need to be directed to bring on the
feared event under conditions where mastery is not required.

What might be some specific tasks and explanations
that could be used to implement this solution shift? The girl
could be instructed to speak publicly but under some very
different conditions than she is used to. She would be asked
to announce before she began her speech that she was extremely nervous and that her anxiety would probably over-
whelm her. This prescribed task amounts to a complete
reversal of the type of solution she has attempted so far.
Rather than attempting to conceal her fear, she is directed to
advertise it. Of course, given her beliefs, this would probably
not be something the girl would be willing to try unless she
got an explanation that made it acceptable. This is precisely
where the ability to use a person's language and beliefs is so
important. One tack that might be used could be to gently
upbraid the girl for taking her fears too lightly, and to direct
her, as a first step, to consider that she needs to more fully
understand the actual fears associated with public speaking.
To become more in touch with these fears, she needs to
explore them more deliberately and systematically. This might
be done by having her go out of her way to answer a question
in class or to make a brief announcement. However, the girl
would be instructed that these speaking assignments were to
be carried out under very different conditions from what she
was used to. In these cases also, she was to preface her speaking by the announcement that she was extremely nervous and
would probably not be able to finish.

A second rationale regularly used for this particular
type of reverse thrust appears in the cases of Milton Erickson
(Erickson and Rossi, 1979) as well as of Fisch, Weakland, and
Segal (1982). The rationale consists of instructing a person to

put himself into the fear-inducing situation not to master it, but merely to develop more of a tolerance to the fear. Fisch and his associates reported using this rationale with a young man who had a fear of being rejected by the opposite sex. The young man was instructed to maximize his chances of rejection deliberately by going to a place where people meet, picking out the most desirable young woman, and approaching her by saying that he would like to get to know her better but was very shy talking with women. He was told that under these circumstances he was likely to be rejected, and even if by some chance he was not rejected, he was not to take her out again or see her since the prime purpose of the assignment was to make him more immune to the impact of rejection, not to meet women.

The solution shift underpinning each of these strategies consists of exposing the person to the feared task while restraining him from successfully mastering it. This response is exactly opposite to the person's usual method (which consists of avoiding the feared task while pushing himself to master it). This solution shift is implemented by prescribing specific transactions in which it is to be performed. In addition, a rationale is provided that makes executing those steps more acceptable to those involved. This solution shift would probably be strongly resisted if it were presented without specific, carefully thought-out steps and explanations of those steps. Planning how to get those involved to implement a solution shift in their everyday life is an important part of intervention planning.

Because people are known to learn new ways of behaving by trying on new behaviors, the practitioner must think in specific transactional terms to change what people say and do in trying to resolve a problem. As illustrated by the example of the young girl anxious about speaking before the class, simply telling someone to stop doing certain things is insufficient to alter problem-maintaining responses. What is needed is the creation of another set of responses that are incompatible with the first and that could be performed in place of the original behavior.

To construct such steps it often helps to consider what specific behaviors are incompatible with the person's current solution effort. For example, Fisch, Weakland, and Segal (1982) suggest that the practitioner ask herself, What actions could the person take that would be the greatest departure from his previous way of responding to the problem? What actions seem most central in the interactional patterns around the problem? Finally, what actions would seem to be most easily incorporated into the person's everyday regimen? Whatever ideas come to mind should be evaluated in terms of these criteria. For example, do these actions involve transactions that occur frequently? Next, which action would be most easy to convince the person to try? Let us consider how the steps designed for the following case met these criteria.

Connie, a seventh-grade girl, was leaving her science class almost every day because she was upset by her science teacher, whom she described as "picking on me." Connie's mother, a single parent, had allowed her daughter to remove herself from the class and stay with her when she became too upset. This very same pattern had happened the year before. In talking with Connie's mother, it became evident that she was reluctant to ask her daughter to stay in a distasteful class. So she had responded by suggesting that if Connie could, she should stay in class. This indirect request was repeatedly met by a veiled refusal from Connie, who stated that she had to leave the class because she was too upset and that she would stay if she could, but somehow she could not.

To create a shift in this way of responding to the problem, a solution shift was formulated that involved only Connie's mother. Because she obviously wanted to ask for her daughter's compliance in attending the class but somehow felt she could not, her response was shifted to making a direct rather than an indirect request of her daughter to attend class even if it appeared arbitrary. This was done by first planning specific ways in which to shift her response in the transactions around the girl's leaving class. Five specific response changes were formulated. Mother was to announce to Connie that she was to remain in class even if she cried; that she could not call home for someone to come to get her unless her fever was 100 degrees; that if she went home sick or stayed home sick, she was to stay in her bed with no TV, radio, phone calls, or visitors, and no talking with her mother about the problem at school; that if she complained to her mother about the upsetting class in the morning on the way to school, she would have to ride the school bus to school the next day; and that she could not change from the class she disliked as her mother would not permit it.

Because these steps represented a radical departure from the way Connie's mother had responded before, it was most important to persuade the mother to carry out these actions. To do this, a rationale was developed based on the mother's benevolent concern for her child. Because Connie's mother had taken the position of not wanting to force her daughter to do something that she wasn't happy doing, the counselor used this position in her rationale. She redefined the mother's benevolence as unwittingly hurtful to her daughter and, conversely, defined what the mother saw as hurtful as beneficial to the girl. This rationale was presented in the following way:

Counselor: After looking into the situation with the science class and talking with Connie as well as you, Mrs. Tompkins, I believe that I'm getting much clearer on the cause of your daughter's unhappiness and poor adjustment to school.

Mother: You are?

Counselor: Yes, I checked out the science class situation, and I've discovered that Mr. Jobson, Connie's science teacher, does not appear to be unduly mean to Connie. So I've realized that something else much deeper is at stake here.

Mother: What do you mean?

Counselor: It seems from what Connie has told me that she fears, whether this is true or not, that she has become the major center of your life, and that you cannot make it without her there closely involved with you. That you readily reschedule and reorder your life around hers, so much so that, from her perspective, she sees you as not having a life separate from hers.

Mother: I don't know about that!

Counselor: Well, of course her beliefs may not fit reality. But she seems to fear greatly that you cannot make it without her in your life. And what is very troublesome about this fear is that it seems to hold her back from risking moving away from you and showing a real liking for school.

Mother: But how have I given her this idea?

Counselor: This may be hard to understand, but, regrettably, it seems that Connie is interpreting all your efforts to be loving and understanding when she is having a hard time in class as your not being able to live without her. Consequently, your efforts of being understanding when she is having a hard time in class are actually having a destructive effect.

Mother: Destructive?

Counselor: Yes, she needs to be reassured that you can make it on your own, that she does not need to be around you every minute for you to feel your life has meaning.

Mother: But how can I do this?

Counselor: One way you could do this is by making it clear to her that you don't need her to constantly prove she likes being with you more than being in school, that she can be in school, that you insist on it and, if need be, will impose consequences if she fails to oblige you.

Mother: I don't know. She seems to be so upset by that teacher.

Counselor: Well, perhaps I am asking too much of you. I guess I only dared to ask because I have felt you willing to make sacrifices if they could benefit your daughter. But of course, you may not want to bother to do what I am suggesting. After all, your daughter has not been that rewarding to you, and you are entitled to take the easy path by continuing what you are doing.

This rationale did serve to motivate Connie's mother to set up the rules then proposed. Although she announced these rules to Connie and the school staff, there followed three more weeks of Connie having intense crying spells and severe upsets in the morning before school, and there were many phone calls from Connie's mother to the counselor. The phone calls were met by the counselor with statements designed to cement the mother's commitment to the direct requests she had made earlier, such as, "I knew this would be very hard, perhaps I'm asking too much of you" and "The one thing Connie really needs is proof that you are willing to not have her be home with you each day. It might be easier to just give up, as she certainly hasn't always treated you very lovingly." These statements helped the mother to hold to her original demands. After about three weeks, Connie stopped regularly pressuring her mother to allow her to leave the class.

In situations such as the one depicted above, one person typically feels inconvenienced by or responsible for another person's behavior. However, he often makes a request of that person indirectly because of his belief that a direct request cannot be made. Such situations become persistent problems the more that external cues suggest that the person avoiding making a direct request needs to make one. The solution shift required in this type of problem is to direct the person who is wanting to ask for something but avoiding doing so to ask directly even if the request appears arbitrary.

As illustrated in the above case, once the practitioner has formulated particular steps that implement the required solution shift, a method for persuading the person involved to try out these steps is necessary. This is where knowing the person's belief system is important. Using the person's existing beliefs about the problem, a rationale can be formulated that makes executing the shift in behavior more palatable. For example, Connie's mother would have been unlikely to shift her way of responding to Connie leaving class along the lines suggested if this had been presented as "showing her daughter that she, the mother, is the boss." The mother did comply, however, when those suggested changes were explained as "supplying evidence that her fears that you can't live without her are ungrounded." In a similar vein, a teacher who views one of her students as troubled is not likely to follow the suggestion that she set certain clear behavioral limits if it is presented with the explanation that she "needs to get tough with him." The teacher might comply, however, if the suggested change in her behavior toward the student were explained as "supplying structure to his otherwise disorganized life." By contrast, a teacher exasperated with a student she believes to be bad is more likely to accept a suggestion framed as a way of "getting control over him or getting him to respect your authority" than one framed as "helping him."

To effectively build explanations that fit the belief structure of those involved, the practitioner needs to develop the ability to restructure links between certain observable facts and the meanings given to those facts. Reframing is an important tool for doing this. Through reframing, new meanings can be associated with facts that previously had been associated with other meanings. "By reframing the conceptual and/or emotional setting or viewpoint in relation to which a situation is experienced, a new meaning is attributed to a set of facts. This new meaning fits the facts of the same concrete situation equally well or better, but carries a radically different emotional meaning with it" (Watzlawick, Weakland, and Fisch, 1974, p. 95).

Many different clinicians routinely build new frames in order to increase certain behaviors and decrease others (Haley, 1973, 1984; Madanes, 1981; Erickson and Rossi, 1979; Watzlawick, Weakland, and Fisch, 1974). Such reframing may involve changing the type of attributions, evaluations, or conclusions assigned to a particular set of facts (O'Hanlon, 1987). One can change attributions of intention, motive, or function ("He does that just to get my goat" or "I must need to put myself down"); attributions of cause ("He made me mess up" personal characteristics ("He's just lazy" or "I think I'm depressed"). Reframing can also be used to modify judgments of the worth of something or someone ("That's not as important right now" or "It was a significant discovery I made") or modify conclusions drawn from a particular action ("Doing that indicates she was afraid you could not make it without her"). In the following case, as in most brief strategic intervention, reframing was used to redefine the nature of the tasks prescribed to the person demonstrating the problem.

This case involved a ninth-grade boy who was fearful of stammering. The boy was instructed to deliberately bring on the stammering in order to observe it adequately and determine which words he stuttered on. The solution shift followed was to reverse the person's basic response thrust from trying to overcome the problem by forcing a good performance to attempting to overcome the problem by consciously planning a bad performance. The boy was instructed to choose a particular time when he would stammer on certain syllables or words or with particular people.

Obviously, such a directive had little likelihood of being followed unless it was presented with a rationale that would make it appear reasonable. Erickson and Rossi (1979) and Fisch, Weakland, and Segal (1982) used two related rationales for dealing with such involuntary performance problems. In both, the person was instructed to fail in his performance, but for different reasons. The first reason was that because important information was still missing that could be used to help figure out what to do about the problem, it was important to bring on the problem for diagnostic purposes. Obviously, only the person with the problem can provide this information by deliberately bringing on the symptom and planning adequately for its occurrence. The second reason was that the symptomatic behavior must be brought on as a beginning step toward its eventual control. This latter explanation was what was suggested to the ninth-grade boy. The practitioner told him, "As a first step for your determining when the symptom is to come and when to go, for you to bring it under your control, you must bring it on."

This was said prior to suggesting he choose particular words he would stammer on. After a couple of days the boy reported a decrease in his stammering. Why did this work?

In this case a normal performance fluctuation was defined as a problem and steps were taken to correct it through forcing a performance that could only occur spontaneously. Telling the boy to stop trying so hard would not work for several reasons. First, the student believed that things would become even worse if he did not continue his efforts to try not to stammer. Second, telling him to stop trying would only make him even more aware of the situation he was trying to correct. Finally, trying to not do something is always harder than trying to do something. For all these reasons, the tack taken was to direct the boy to perform a behavior that was incompatible with the behavior he wished to stop.

In summary, it can be seen from the cases reported in this chapter as well as in earlier chapters that a specific intervention plan must be designed for each case that interrupts the current problem-maintaining behavior of the problem-bearer and others with whom she is involved. To tailor a specific intervention plan to the needs of a situation, three elements are always necessary: A solution shift must be identified, specific steps to implement that shift must be constructed, and a rationale making such steps more attractive must be presented. As a next step, the practitioner must consider whether this intervention plan is having an impact on problem behavior. This is usually done by monitoring and evaluating the actions of those involved. In the next chapter, methods related to this step are considered.

CHAPTER 8

Monitoring and Evaluating the Intervention Effort

How does the practitioner know if his efforts to change interactions around a student problem are having a positive
impact? When does he decide an intervention can be ended?
How does he reach the conclusion that another intervention
approach is more appropriate? Finally, how does he determine
to what extent he has been successful? Obviously, personal
conviction or faith in the value of brief strategic intervention
is not enough. It is necessary for the practitioner to gather
solid evidence concerning the impact of his intervention
efforts. In this chapter, procedures for gathering such evidence
are described. Initially, various reasons for monitoring and
evaluating the change effort are presented. This is followed
by a discussion of the general rules to be met in designing
a monitoring strategy. Evidence for the effectiveness of brief
strategic intervention is reported next, along with specific
methods for implementing a case-monitoring strategy.

There are a number of different reasons for the practitioner to monitor and evaluate her efforts to change problematic student behavior. First, the practitioner may want to
know whether what she is doing at a particular stage of the
intervention is having an impact. For example, are the problem behaviors being modified and in what way? Second, the
practitioner may want to determine whether enough change
has occurred to merit ending the change effort. Finally, she
may be interested in determining if the changes reported are

enduring. Monitoring and evaluating the intervention effort can answer such questions. Although school helping professionals typically gather such information through informal feedback from parents, teachers, and others involved in the problem, using more formal methods has several advantages. First, it allows the practitioner to learn from her own practice in a more systematic fashion. Second, it enhances her accountability. Third, it advances clinical practice. Let us look more closely at each of these possible advantages.

Most practitioners are quite interested in maximizing what they learn from applying an approach in one case and transferring this learning to other case situations. To do this, the practitioner needs to know which kinds of cases an approach works on, what the essential elements are that make the intervention successful, how long she needs to apply the intervention strategy to get results, and whether the changes reported are lasting. Systematically collecting information about the nature of the presenting problem (or problem/solution cycle) and the progress made can help answer such questions.

In addition to learning more about the problem situation, the practitioner may also be interested in evaluating the intervention process itself. For example, the practitioner may wonder whether her intervention activities are targeting the most relevant features of the problem situation, how much intervention is necessary, and whether what she thinks is being delivered in the way of treatment is, in fact, being delivered. Collecting evidence over time about the characteristics of the problem situation, the nature of the intervention, and any changes in the situation can help the practitioner answer these questions.

In addition to satisfying their own curiosity as to whether an intervention is having an impact, most practitioners are experiencing increased pressure to supply evidence that their interventions actually help students. Many practitioners are now routinely asked about the effectiveness of their counseling procedures and are required to document their effectiveness. Although this trend toward accountability is due, in large part, to the greatly increased costs of educational services in general and mental health services in particular, more is at stake than cost containment. There is also a genuine desire to ensure that the quality of the services provided is up to par. Having some evidence concerning which intervention efforts are the most appropriate, which pose the least risk (for example, of negatively labeling a student), and which are the least intrusive can help to ensure that an adequate adequate quality of service is being provided.

Regrettably, there is little objective evidence as to the appropriateness, effectiveness, and safety of the various intervention procedures now used routinely in the schools. In addition, many studies of school-based interventions have been faulted for basic design limitations such as failing to clearly define the intervention, using a diffusely described population, and attempting to assess progress by using a global judgment of outcome. Is it any wonder that most school helping professionals experiment with new intervention techniques because of their appeal rather than because of hard evidence in their favor?

Obviously, there is a need for research that carefully specifies the intervention applied and its functional outcomes and collects pertinent evidence over time. There has been interest in single-case design approaches where the research strategy is to carefully specify the intervention elements in terms of one case and then to measure the functional outcomes on a repeated basis. Using a time-series methodology, individual cases are analyzed on an intensive basis and the intervention procedure is repeated over a number of cases presenting the same problem. This forms a clinical replication series in which practitioners using a well-specified intervention accumulate a series of cases presenting the same problem.

Barlow, Hayes, and Nelson (1984, p. 62) describe the overriding emphasis in this strategy as "the return to the paramount importance of the individual in any research process concerned with developing techniques and procedures in the general area of behavior change." This new research approach contrasts markedly with the traditional between-groups experimental methodology familiar to most school helping professionals. Until recently, most evaluation studies of counseling or educational practice were based on this traditional research model. The assumptions underpinning this model were that large numbers of individuals were available who were relatively homogeneous in terms of key client characteristics, that practitioners would not alter treatment strategies if it became obvious that it would be beneficial to the client, and that treatment was to be continued or discontinued irrespective of client progress (Barlow, Hayes, and Nelson, 1984). Because these assumptions could often not be met in practice, practitioners have been inhibited in conducting research or have reported research that did not meet the criteria for good research established in the traditional model. Now, single-case experimental designs offer the practitioner a methodology for determining how effective and efficient a specific intervention is on an individual-client basis.

Although this research approach provides a method by which the practitioner can evaluate the impact of her own intervention, to use this approach effectively certain rules must be followed for describing and monitoring the intervention process.

Hersen and Barlow (1976) specify a number of rules of good practice in monitoring and evaluating the clinical intervention process. These include describing client characteristics and selection procedures, describing the intervention procedures used in great detail, using reliable and nonreactive change measures, and analyzing failures as well as successes.

To provide the most useful information for himself and others, the practitioner needs to carefully describe the nature of the problem in which he is intervening, and the behaviors targeted for change. In addition, it is also useful to describe key background factors considered relevant. Such information gathering can be a part of one's preliminary case assessment.

The procedures followed in carrying out an intervention need to be described in enough detail so that other practitioners could apply them. Conveying the essential features of the intervention clearly helps to reveal those elements that are responsible for any change in client behavior.

The measures selected to assess client change must be both reliable and nonreactive. Thus, the practitioner needs to choose measures that will reliably index any success or failure resulting from the intervention. In addition, the practitioner needs to employ information-gathering techniques that are broad enough to provide a means for monitoring the overall functioning and well-being of the people involved.

Unlike other evaluation strategies, clinical replication requires that the practitioner analyze not only whether the client improves, but how and to what extent he improves. It may be that the client improves only to a limited extent. This, according to Hersen and Barlow (1976), is quite useful in providing answers as to what works and what does not work in a clinical intervention. Thus, the practitioner will be interested in determining whether the client did not show enough improvement to be clinically significant, deteriorated as a result of the intervention, or made significant improvement, and in analyzing the reasons for these outcomes.

Regrettably, these rules of good practice have been applied on a haphazard basis in much of the available brief strategic research literature. Indeed, much remains to be discovered about the effective use of brief strategic intervention with school-related problems. Although there have been a significant number of articles and books that describe cases in which this approach has been employed, the published experimental literature is scant. Until recently, two types of evidence of effectiveness have been available. The first type consists of anecdotal accounts by both school and non-school mental health professionals regarding the application of this approach with children and adolescents presenting behavior problems. O'Connor (1983), for example, a psychologist employed by a mental health center, reported resolution of the presenting problem using this approach in the treatment of a ten-year-old boy who obsessively feared he would vomit at school and at home. Wetchler (1986), a family therapist in private practice, also reported positive results from applying this approach in working with two different cases involving seventh-grade boys. In one case, the student had temper outbursts at school; in the other, the student refused to do home-work. Reports from the Brief Therapy Center at MRI have also reported successful outcomes with school-aged youth. Weakland (1977b), for example, reported working with a fifteen-year-old boy who was doing poor work in school and was truant. Fisch (1977) reported using these methods with a twelve-year-old neurologically impaired boy who was having trouble socializing with other children at home and at school, and with a fifteen-year-old girl (Fisch, Weakland, and Segal, 1982) who refused to accept any direction from her parents.

In addition to these non-school helping professionals, a number of school professionals have reported successful outcomes using this approach with children and adolescents. Williams, a school counselor, and Weeks, her clinical supervisor, reported positive outcomes in six different cases involving seventh-, eighth-, and ninth-grade students in which brief strategic methods were used (Williams and Weeks, 1984). Wiswell (1986), a school counselor, also reported success in working with a sixth-grade student who had gotten into a cycle of chronic lying about why his homework was not completed. Finally, Power and Bartholomew (1988), two school psychologists who treated a fourth-grade boy for poor academic performance and facial tics, indicated successful remission of the tic behavior and significant academic gains using these methods.

In each of these reports, the impact of the intervention was monitored on an informal basis with the solicitation of feedback by the helping professional about change in the problem behaviors. Although a strength in these reports is the careful detailing of the intervention employed and the characteristics of the problem situation, a major weakness is the informal manner in which change data were collected and the focus on only successes.

Two exceptions to this statement are provided by the accounts of Hsai (1984), who worked with a twelve-year-old girl who refused to attend school, and Zarske (1982), who was involved in the treatment of a cerebral palsied child who demonstrated temper tantrums. These two studies begin to meet some of the rules of good practice described above. In the Hsai study the girl's school attendance was systematically monitored over a nine-week period. In the Zarske study the parents were instructed to chart the frequency, duration, and location of the child's tantrums on a daily basis and follow-up data were collected at one- and two-month intervals. These studies go well beyond the vast majority of the studies reported above in providing some form of experimental measurement to demonstrate treatment effectiveness.

A second type of effort evaluating the effectiveness of brief strategic techniques has been in the form of large, uncontrolled group studies assessing the outcome of participation in brief strategic therapy. Two such studies have been reported to date. In one, Weakland and his associates at the Brief Therapy Center of the MRI evaluated their work over six years with all individuals seen (Weakland, Fisch, Watzlawick, and Bodin, 1974). A total of 97 individual, marital, and family cases were handled (involving 236 people in all). A broad socioeconomic range of clients and an equally wide variety of clinical problems, chronic as well as acute, were reported; however, no specific description of the sample was provided. Cases came from many different referral sources and included individuals from five to sixty years of age. They involved a maximum of ten one-hour sessions, usually scheduled at weekly intervals. In the main, treatment attempted to achieve "limited but significant goals in alleviating the major complaint of the patients" (p. 142). According to this objective, about three-quarters of the cases were seen as culminating successfully.

The authors drew their conclusions about each case on the basis of client interviews conducted by a nonparticipating therapist approximately three months after treatment. In this follow-up interview, clients were asked four questions pertaining to the alleviation of their problem and the occurrence of constructive behavioral change. The first question was, When you first came to the Brief Therapy Center, you were concerned about (evaluator supplied presenting complaint from initial intake record); is your concern now the same,

greater, or less? (If different, the evaluator asked for an illus-
trative example.) The second question was, Since you were
last seen at the Brief Therapy Center have any other problems arisen? The third was, Since you were last seen at the
Brief Therapy Center, have any other problems been resolved
that were not dealt with at the center? The last was, Have
you secured any further therapy? According to Bodin (1981),
responses to these questions were not cleanly categorizable
since sometimes the clinician's goal was approached and
much improvement was evident but without complete resolution of the problem, while other times the treatment goal had
not been formulated in sufficiently explicit and concrete terms
to permit any check on its achievement. In still other cases,
either the planned change occurred but did not bring relief,
or the planned change did not occur although relief came
anyway. Because of this lack of clarity, responses to these questions led to a threefold classification of results: 40 percent of
the cases (39 out of the 97) obtained complete relief from the
dominant problem; 32 percent (31 out of the 97) demonstrated
significant though incomplete improvement, and the remaining 28 percent (27 out of 97) showed little or no change in the
main problem (that is, treatment was deemed a failure).

Although this improvement rate of 72 percent is very
impressive, especially since the average number of sessions
per case was only seven, this study does not meet the criteria
for good research either as a traditional comparison group
study or as a clinical replication series. First, this was not a
controlled study and thus is hard to fit within a traditional
comparison group framework. Secondly, it falls short as a
clinical replication series because the client population was
diffusely described and not screened in any systematic way,
the treatment procedures were not well specified, the outcome
criteria were symptom-focused and unidimensional, and the
study failed to take into account the possibility of certain
extratherapy variables which may in some cases have influenced the results.

In a subsequent study with the same limitations, Bodin
(1981) reported an 82 percent success rate in evaluating the

effectiveness of MRI brief intervention with 124 police depu-
ties and their families. In a two-year contract with a local
police department, psychotherapy services were evaluated
using a similar procedure to that described above. Bodin
reported that in thirty of the thirty-four cases closed the first
year, primary objectives were met. In the second year, sixty
of the seventy-six cases were closed with the primary goals
reported met.

Thus, much remains to be discovered about the effective use of brief strategic intervention in the schools. Let us
consider some of the steps practitioners might take to remedy
this situation. To monitor and evaluate the impact of a brief
strategic intervention effort, the practitioner will need to: state
the problem in specific enough terms that any change can
be concretely measured, decide what aspect of the problem
should be targeted for intervention and assessment, plan to
collect multiple measures of changed behavior from various
people involved with the complaint, consider whether the
measures selected are both sensitive and meaningful enough
to register changes in the targeted behaviors if used on a
repeated basis, and collect evidence from these various measures over time, comparing the evidence from these readings
at different points in time (Barlow, Hayes, and Nelson, 1984).

Because the brief strategic practitioner stays focused on
changing the presenting complaint, change in the status of
this complaint can serve as an excellent marker of change. It
is, however, more difficult that one might imagine, even in
this approach, to get a concrete description of the presenting
complaint that can be translated into a measurable therapeutic objective. This is because, as mentioned in Chapter Five,
most people tend to think in somewhat global terms about
their problem. There are several strategies the practitioner
can use, however, to help people translate their global descriptions into more specific, measurable behaviors that can serve
as markers for change. One strategy is to ask the client what
she would consider acceptable evidence of having attained
the desired goal. The practitioner can ask questions such as
"How would you know when we were starting to be success-

ful here?" "What might be one small sign to indicate that things are beginning to change in the desired direction?" For example, a teacher consulting a school psychologist about a fifth-grade student who fails to complete his homework and makes frequent, vociferous excuses to avoid completing it, might say that acceptable evidence of improvement would be fewer excuses for incomplete assignments and completion of all assignments on a consistent basis. (See Exhibits 2 and 3 for samples of simple questionnaires the psychologist might use to collect information about the status of the problem and improvement in it over time.)

Another possible strategy the psychologist might use in helping a teacher define the problem in more specific terms would be to ask the teacher, If three wishes could be granted, what would they be? In this case, the teacher might say her wishes were that the student would do his assignments without having her remind him, that she would not have to put up with the student's excuses, and that she would be able to spend her time engaged in more positive exchanges with the student.

An alternative strategy might be to first ask the teacher to describe a typical day (or week) in order to get a picture of the current problem behavior in all its manifestations. Next, the teacher could be asked to describe an ideal day (or week) to establish what might be the intervention goals. In this case, the teacher might state that on an ideal day she might not have to engage in any defensive conversation with the student about homework assignments, and the student would turn in all his assignments. These statements could then be translated into specific change markers.

Another common strategy that could be used to develop a more specific picture of possible treatment goals and outcomes is goal-attainment scaling (Kiresuk and Sherman, 1968). In this approach, the psychologist would solicit a statement from the teacher of the desired goal for the intervention and then creates a scale composed of a series of likely intervention outcomes varying from least favorable through most likely to most favorable. An objective event would be tied to

Exhibit 2. Individualized Problem Description.

Are there specific negative behaviors you would like to see the student do less of? Or are there specific positive behaviors you would like to see the student do more of? Please describe two specific problem areas for which you want help.

Problem Area 1. Describe the problem (that is, what exactly does the student do or say that presents a problem?).

In your opinion what would be specific evidence (that is, things the student is doing or saying) to indicate that this problem behavior was starting to change?

Problem Area 2. Describe the problem (that is, what exactly does the student do or say that presents a problem?).

In your opinion what would be specific evidence (that is, things the student is doing or saying) to indicate that this problem behavior was starting to change?

Exhibit 3. Individualized Problem Improvement Scales.

Please rate whether the student has improved in the two specific problem areas on which you felt this student needed help.

Problem Area 1. Problem was:

To what extent has the student changed in this problem area? Choose one of the following:
(1) Is much worse
(2) Is somewhat worse
(3) Is neither better nor worse
(4) Is somewhat better
(5) Is much better

Problem Area 2. Problem was:

To what extent has the student changed in this problem area? Choose one of the following:
(1) Is much worse
(2) Is somewhat worse
(3) Is neither better nor worse
(4) Is somewhat better
(5) Is much better

Additional Help Questions

Have you had to seek additional help in resolving this student's problem(s) during the past two weeks? If so, what exactly have you had to do? What other help do you think may be necessary?

each scale outcome. For example, in the case above, the goal was the boy completing homework. The least favorable outcome might be "completes none of his homework and argues about why he does not have his work"; the most likely outcome might be "completes most homework but routinely argues about the need to do it"; and the most favorable outcome might be "completes all homework and does not engage in undue argument about completing it."

With this as well as with the preceding strategies, one has the task of taking long-term or global goals and translating them into more specific, measurable behavioral indicators. This often involves specifying partial or instrumental goals. Nelsen (1981) and others (Barlow, Hayes, and Nelson, 1984) define partial goals as involving part of a final goal, while instrumental goals involve doing something that builds up the skills needed to accomplish the final goal. For example, in the case above, the long-term goal might be for the student to complete his homework with no undue attention or altercation. Partial goals, which would be insufficient in and of themselves but would lead indirectly to the final goal, might be that the boy would write down all assignments and not make excuses for incomplete work.

In summary, the first step in one's monitoring effort is to specify the problem and intervention goal in terms of specific behaviors that can be measured. This can be accomplished through development of specific interview questions, partial or instrumental goals, and/or a goal-attainment scale.

Most school-related complaints are complex enough to involve several problem areas. For example, in the case above, the student not only did not complete his homework, he also frequently made noises in class that were irritating to his classmates and baited other students into altercations with him and then denied doing so. Although the teacher might feel that each of these problem behaviors needs to be eliminated, it would be unrealistic to assume that change in all these behaviors could be accomplished at the same time. Even though each of these behaviors is characteristic of a student engaged in a power struggle with others, targeting one behavior at a time for change is usually necessary. Thus, while the psychologist in this case will want to get all relevant problem areas identified and take quantified measure of their occurrence, she will then ask the teacher to prioritize among them to establish an initial direction. Subsequently, with each problem area prioritized, it will be necessary to identify several partial or instrumental behaviors so that evidence can be collected concerning their occurrence.

The practitioner should plan to obtain several different measures of the status of the problem behaviors from several vantage points. For example, the psychologist working with the complaint about the fifth-grade boy described above might plan to obtain measures from the teacher's and the parents' perspectives. The psychologist could ask the teacher to keep a log of the frequency with which the boy completed homework assigned each day. A second behavior that might be tallied by the teacher might be the frequency with which the boy gave excuses for missed or incomplete assignments, or argued about the assignments. An alternative approach might be to ask the teacher to log not only the above behaviors but the consequences that occurred at school as a result of them (for example, the frequency of "smiley" or "frown" faces earned each day for complete or incomplete work, or times kept in at recess to finish work). In addition, the psychologist may wish to have the boy's parents keep a record of the teacher's report of complete or incomplete work and the consequences for incomplete work meted out during each week at home. The value of having this kind of information collected by both the teacher and parent is that it describes not only changes in status of the targeted problem behaviors but also the implementation of the intervention procedures.

The above examples illustrate using different vantage points to measure the same or related behavioral content. In addition to the *source* changing, the *content* of the measurement may need to vary, along with a corresponding change in measurement mode. For example, some types of problem situations, such as anxiety or depressive states, may require measuring changes in the status of both client cognitions and actions. Self-reporting modes of measurement are often useful in measuring cognitive content (for example, What are you

thinking about the current problem situation?), while observational modes of measurement (for example, a frequency
count of specific behaviors) are more useful for measuring
changes in action. In light of these considerations, using
multiple measures to assess progress in resolving a client's
complaint helps clarify the nature of any progress made and
the source of that progress.

Instead of just measuring a change in problem status
before and after the intervention, the practitioner should consider collecting measures during the intervention as well. This
is useful for several reasons. First, collecting such measures
during treatment provides feedback on how effectively an
intervention is working at a particular time during the intervention process. If the practitioner does not get the progress
expected, she may wish to change some of the elements in the
intervention. Second, getting measures of key indices during
the intervention process may provide much more information
about features of the problem-solution cycle that need to be
altered.

Deciding to gather evidence on a repeated basis over
time has a significant impact on the kinds of measures
selected for monitoring the impact of the intervention effort.
Some measures may be useful for getting a broad general
picture of the problem behavior. Such molar measures, as
they're called (Barlow, Hayes, and Nelson, 1984), provide a
clear picture of the relative status of the problem behavior in
the student in question and also often reveal how much the
student differs from others his age on these behavioral indices.
Numerous inventories exist measuring the frequency of occurrence of a wide array of problem behaviors in students as
reported from the perspective of the student, his parents, and
the school staff.

There are also a considerable number of instruments
available measuring one particular target problem and its
manifestations—for example, the Taylor Manifest Anxiety
Scale or the State-Trait Anxiety Scale for Children. Developers
of these instruments have usually taken great care to provide
evidence of good construct validity and reliability. While these
instruments are quite useful in describing the extensiveness

of the problem from varying viewpoints, they are usually not designed to be very sensitive to any slight progress toward therapeutic goals. Thus, such measures may be useful to describe the nature of the problem, to plot gross changes such as might occur two or three times over a year (for example, at the beginning and end of treatment in a three-month period, and again three months later during a follow-up measure). However, these types of measure are usually insensitive to small, gradual changes.

To measure very small changes in client status, more specific, or molecular, measures are needed. Such measures should be designed to be both precise and sensitive to any relevant client changes. Returning to the example of the fifth grader, the psychologist may ascertain that a willingness to assume responsibility for homework tasks is the problem. Specific behaviors that might be targeted for change and assessed on a daily basis by means of a teacher or parent checklist might include taking down complete homework instructions in an assignment pad or taking home all materials necessary to complete an assignment. Because these behaviors might change even though the presenting complaint remained unaltered, molecular measures should not be the only type of measure used. Both global (molar) measures of change and specific (molecular) measures need to be used.

A practitioner interested in evaluating her effectiveness should plan to take repeated measures over time of a particular problem situation. Collecting such measures early will serve as a baseline against which to compare the effects of one's interventions. In addition, measuring the targeted behaviors several times over the course of an intervention allows one to see if changes in specific elements of the intervention are related to behavioral changes.

But what does the practitioner do with all this information? A convenient way to store and interpret repeated measurement is to graph the data (Hersen and Barlow, 1976; Parsonson and Baer, 1978). The time elapsing from the baseline measurement through the next measurement points can be indexed on the horizontal axis, and the degree of change can be indexed on the vertical axis. (Obviously, the unit of change must be appropriate for the type of measure used.) One might even consider asking those involved in the problem (such as teachers or parents) to follow this recordkeeping procedure.

Let us illustrate how these steps were put into practice by the psychologist working with Tony, the fifth grader referred to above who did not complete homework on a regular basis. During the first week of school, Tony's teacher, Mrs. Jarvis, requested a meeting with the psychologist to discuss the boy's situation. In response to a series of four open-ended sentences, Tony had written he was quite unhappy with school and felt like killing himself. Mrs. Jarvis was quite worried. However, in talking with Tony privately, Mrs. Jarvis reported that Tony did not act unduly depressed but instead reported being unhappy with the amount of homework he was given and the lack of opportunity he had to play with other kids at school. He talked in an overly dramatic way, appeared unwilling to take much direction from Mrs. Jarvis, and seemed unaware of how his behavior with other students (which often consisted of teasing them or baiting them into a fight) alienated them from him.

Worried about his threat to kill himself, Mrs. Jarvis decided she would work on making him aware of how what he did in the classroom bothered the other students and made them steer clear of him. She obviously believed that Tony was upset and needed careful and concerned handling. She and Tony worked out a signaling system in which she pulled her ear to signal him to stop three behaviors that irritated other students. These were making odd noises when students were to work quietly at their desks, getting up and wandering around the room, and touching other students. He was to immediately stop the behaviors when she gave the signal. If he did so, as his reward he could give a talk before the class for ten minutes on Friday. (Tony was incredibly loquacious so that getting people to listen to him was just to his liking.) Mrs. Jarvis agreed to keep track by means of a daily record sheet of the frequency with which she reminded him concerning the three actions over three weeks. Tony also had a record sheet for keeping track of his actions in the three categories. If he had no more than three goofs, he would be allowed to have his reward.

The first week Tony did exceptionally well; he goofed up by persisting in the actions only three times and got an opportunity to speak before the class. By the second week, however, Mrs. Jarvis reported that Tony seemed to be going out of his way to test whether she was on her toes and would signal him. She acknowledged that she had begun to feel the signaling system was serving as a way to get her attention, as he had not decreased the problematic behaviors very much and only discontinued them when she signaled him. In addition, Tony was not completing his classwork or his homework assignments. Thus, Mrs. Jarvis felt, the focus of the intervention effort needed to be redirected.

As a baseline, the psychologist requested that Mrs. Jarvis fill out a Teacher Observation Checklist (a global rating scale of various positive and negative classroom behaviors). In addition, to get a clearer view of what was now emerging as the problem behaviors as well as to develop some indicators of improvement, the counselor had the teacher complete the Problem Rating Scale (see Exhibit 2). Next, the psychologist and Mrs. Jarvis decided to call in Tony's mother and father to discuss the situation, examine how each person was responding to the problem behaviors, and brainstorm with them about ways of subverting these behaviors.

Interestingly, although Tony's parents seemed quite concerned about Tony's threats to kill himself and about his incomplete schoolwork, they seemed unsure how to respond. They were both easygoing individuals who were used to comforting Tony, an only child, when he was upset and letting him have his way. They seemed quite willing, however, to shift their laissez-faire response at home, especially when it was framed as helping Tony learn what he needed to do in school to succeed. The psychologist, Mrs. Jarvis, and Tony's parents talked at length about Tony's misbehavior. It was decided that Tony would be punished at home by not being allowed to play or watch TV if he came home with a report of having not completed his homework from the night before.

The teacher was to send home a "smiley" face if the homework had been completed, a "frown" face if it had not. The teacher was asked to keep a record of what had and had not been completed in a weekly log. She was told not to remind Tony of his assignments but to deal with him like the other students in her class. If homework was incomplete, a report of what was not complete was to be sent home with the frown face.

The first day into the plan, Tony went home without the necessary books to do his work. Thus he received a frown face for incomplete work. The parents made good on their plan. As it was Friday and his parents had told him he would be kept in the entire weekend if he did not get a smiley face, Tony spent the entire weekend in his room. The following Monday and Tuesday, Mrs. Jarvis reported that Tony was a different person. However, by Wednesday Tony was back to his old practices of not completing his work and disturbing others. In response to Mrs. Jarvis's query as to why he had changed back, Tony announced that he would be allowed to go his Cub Scout meeting because he had earned two smiley faces. It was obvious that Tony was going to do no more than necessary.

Meeting with the parents two days later, Mrs. Jarvis reported that after the Cub Scout meeting Tony went back to his old ways. It was apparent that Cub Scouts was a strong reward—much stronger than just having to stay in his room. So under strong encouragement from the teacher and psychologist, the parents revised the plan to be that Tony had to have a perfect record of completed homework for the entire week (a total of five smiley faces) to be allowed to go to the Cub Scout meeting. Although Tony's parents agreed to this plan, they voiced concern about Tony being given a chance to succeed. They were not aware that the boy, who was quite bright, had succeeded with little effort the previous Monday and Tuesday. Over time, however, it slowly seemed to dawn on Tony's parents that Tony was used to having things his way and would need to be retrained. This became evident when Tony lied to his parents about having homework to do, failed to bring books home, or complained that the teacher had not given the assignment she claimed he did not complete. As Tony's mother and father were confronted with these incidents, they became increasingly firmer in their demands, and Tony began to do his work on a regular basis. Over the following two months, Tony's teacher and mother kept up the charting, and both reported a sharp drop-off (with some ups and downs) in the missed classwork and homework.

At the end of the fourteenth week, the teacher and each parent completed the Individualized Problem Improvement Scale (see Exhibit 3). Comparing their perceptions, they all agreed that Tony's behavior had changed. He was doing much less talking back and maneuvering to get around doing his homework. Tony's mother and father, in particular, felt that while they still had to keep close tabs on him, it appeared that Tony was now accepting the reality of doing his work without fighting it. Interestingly, over the same period, Tony also became involved in the school basketball program—something he had never shown interest in before—and had made two friends of other students involved in that activity.

In summary, there are a number of purposes to be served by monitoring and evaluating one's intervention efforts. One can easily develop a monitoring and evaluation strategy based on a single-case design. However, several rules of good practice need to be considered and incorporated on a routine basis into one's clinical practice. In the next chapters, cases will be described in which brief strategic interventions were developed and monitored. Hopefully, they will provide a further illustration of how intervention development, implementation, and monitoring go hand in hand.

Intervening in
Typical Student Problems

In the past six chapters, I have described the basic steps employed by school professionals implementing a brief strategic approach. Part Three, consisting of Chapters Nine, Ten, and Eleven, illustrates how these steps are implemented in actual school practice. Three different case examples are reported. Chapter Nine describes my work with a young kindergarten student who had temper tantrums at school and at home. Chapter Ten describes my efforts to assist a twelve-year-old boy who stole things in school. Finally, in Chapter Eleven, Patricia Carrow outlines her efforts to help a fifteen-year-old girl who refused to attend school. In each of these chapters, extensive portions of case dialogue are included along with the actual thinking of the helping professional as to why particular moves were made. Hopefully, reading these cases will help in two ways. First, it may make it easier to see how the package of intervention steps comes together in actual practice. Second, seeing the whole array of different efforts made in working with a child may help the reader grasp more readily when this intervention approach should be considered.

CHAPTER 9

A Case of
Persistent Temper Tantrums

In the following case, the mother of Becky, a five-year-old girl who had persistent tantrums at school and at home, was referred by the child's teacher and school principal to me in my role as a psychological consultant for a small, private, church-related school. The child, a kindergartner, was reported to have managed to upset her classmates and her teacher with her tantrums over the four weeks since her enrollment. The teacher reported that the tantrums usually resulted whenever she directly requested that Becky follow her instructions (such as lining up with the class to go to lunch, taking her seat, or engaging in a specific work task). The teacher's repeated urging for Becky to follow her directives often led to the child screaming and kicking out at the teacher. Such temper tantrums ceased only when the teacher backed off and allowed Becky to do what she wished.

The teacher (and principal) had first responded to the tantrums by explaining to Becky what was expected of her, then reprimanding her for her actions and directing her to comply. Since these actions seemed only to intensify the tantrums, the teacher had begun physically removing Becky from

Note: Portions of this chapter are excerpted from Amatea, E. "Brief Systemic Intervention: A Case of Temper Tantrums." *Psychology in the Schools,* 1988, *25,* 174–183. Reprinted here by permission of Clinical Psychology Publishing Company, Inc.

the class and making her sit in a time-out space for an allotted period. This consequence did not seem to deter Becky either. She continued to respond with outbursts at least three or four times a week. Becky's mother had been contacted after her daughter's first outburst, and she had met with the teacher. However, neither she nor the staff had been able to eliminate the problem behavior.

I first asked Becky's mother to come in without her daughter in order to assess her perceptions of the problem and her responses to it. In this initial conference the mother, an attractive young woman in her early thirties, reported being intimidated by Becky's tantrums and concerned that the school would dismiss her if her behavior did not improve. Since this would require moving Becky to a public school that the mother considered inferior, she was anxious to have Becky stop the tantrums. She indicated that she was having similar problems with Becky at home and reported that there had been a number of major changes in the family to which she feared Becky was reacting. The mother told of separating from her husband during the past summer after learning of his affair with another woman and then relocating her family in a new town where she could live closer to her married sister. She was working, and she and her two daughters, Julie, seven, and Becky, five, were currently living with the mother's married sister, the sister's husband, and their two-year-old son. In the following dialogue, a clear picture emerges of the mother's view of her daughter's problem and her response to it.

Psychologist: I appreciate your coming in, Mrs. Carter. I know how hard it must be to get time off from your job to come here. As you know, Becky's teacher recommended that we get together because Becky has had some tantrums in class, which her teacher sees as a problem. But I'm wondering if you see this as a problem?

Mother: Well, I know how difficult Becky can be sometimes. She really can be a handful.

Psychologist: What do you mean exactly?

Mother: Well, I know that she can get upset about doing something, and then there's no budging her.

Psychologist: Is this something about which you've had difficulty with her, too?

Mother: Oh yes, when she gets her mind set about what she is or is not going to do, there's no bucking her.

Psychologist: Can you tell me of a time recently when this happened with you? What happened when she got to the point, as you say, "where there was no bucking her"?

Mother: Well, the other day when we were getting ready for school, she got upset when I didn't have her favorite outfit washed and ready. She yelled and said that she wasn't going to school because of this. I tried to be understanding. After all, it was early in the morning, and she is hard to get moving in the morning.

Psychologist: Tried to be understanding? What do you mean exactly?

Mother: Well, I got out another outfit I thought she would like and told her to calm down and that this outfit would be just as good to wear.

Psychologist: Then what happened?

Mother: She just screamed more and insisted she wouldn't go to school.

Psychologist: What happened then?

Mother: I tried to explain to her that I could not get the dress ready then, but she kept on screaming at me.

Psychologist: Then what happened?

Mother: Well, I know I shouldn't have done this, but I just finally had enough. I slapped her on the behind, and told her that she was to wear the outfit I gave her. She cried all the more then. But I dressed her anyway. We got to school in an awful mood, all of us.

Psychologist: All of us—you mean you and Becky and Julie?

Mother: Yes, we all get miserable when we have a morning like that.

Psychologist: What does Julie do when all this is going on?

Mother: She tries to help me calm Becky down.

Psychologist: And does that work?

Mother: Not really, it just seems to get Becky madder.

Psychologist: So it sounds like when Becky got really mad, the only thing that you could think that might work was to spank her?

Mother: Yes, and I hate myself for reaching that point, but she was making us all late. I know I should have been more patient with her. After all, she has had a lot to go through lately. I shouldn't have lost control. I know she's just reacting to a lot of the changes we have been going through.

Psychologist: Can you tell me about how you think these changes are affecting Becky?

Mother: Well, I've left the girls' dad and moved them down here and in with my sister and her family. I know they've had a lot to adjust to. And Becky was her father's favorite. I know she misses him.

Psychologist: So you think that her upsets are the result of these various changes you have put the girls through?

Mother: Oh yes. I know that Becky has been too small to understand, but she can't help but be upset by all this. I really know I just need to be more patient with her. I haven't wanted to tell the school my personal business, but I'm sure that's why Becky is acting up there. I'm afraid they will think even worse of me if I tell them about the separation. But I also think Mrs. Schroeder [Becky's teacher] is being too hard on her. After all, she is only five.

Becky's mother talked on about her child's teacher. She seemed annoyed with the teacher and complained about her being unbending and insensitive in dealing with Becky. The mother also seemed angry about getting negative reports with the implication that she should do something about the child's behavior. (In an earlier conversation that I had had with the teacher, who did not know of the separation of Becky's parents, the teacher had stated that she thought the mother was not being firm enough and had allowed Becky to have her own way too much.) However, the mother did admit to feeling helpless and frantic over her daughter's tantrums, which occurred at home even more frequently than they did at school (four to five times weekly). She indicated that she responded to the tantrums either by demanding that Becky obey her or, if that did not work, punishing Becky by spanking and scolding her when she did not obey. Becky's mother acknowledged that while neither of these tactics had worked, she did not now how else to control Becky.

Information from this interview led me to several speculations as to how the problem behavior might be being maintained and what might be appropriate as a target for our intervention effort. First, although the mother seemed to view Becky's tantrums as a result of the trauma of the family's separation, both she and the school responded similarly to the tantrums by attempting to control the behavior, even though this appeared to escalate it. Second, the sister's efforts to play mother's helper seemed to further intensify Becky's response. To determine how Becky saw her problem and the responses of others to her, I suggested an individual session with Becky. I did this for several reasons. First, this session would provide me with some important information about how Becky was responding to the situation at home and at school. Second, my meeting with Becky could serve to legitimize my future requests for her mother to respond differently to her.

I saw Becky by herself two days later. She met me with a smile on her face, her blond pigtails bobbing as she walked. She was not hesitant in meeting me and quickly began to talk when I said hello. As we entered my office, she spied some puppets in the corner of the room. She went over to the puppets and picked them up, then saw a dollhouse and moved toward it. She looked around for the dolls (I had several sets of family members) and chose a mother, a father, a girl doll, and another girl doll somewhat smaller than the first. She asked if I would play dolls with her. I agreed and she said I was to be the mommy. When I asked what the mother doll was to be doing, she directed me to put the mother doll in the kitchen, cooking. I said that the mother would be cooking breakfast and calling everyone to come eat. She brought the three other dolls in the kitchen and sat everyone down to eat. Then she had them all get up to go to school. As she had the girls walk upstairs, she saw a rubber alligator, which she grabbed and had enter the house and eat up the older girl doll. I asked her if the remaining little girl doll felt scared. She said no and stopped the play. She then lined up the dolls again—the mother and the two girl dolls (there was no action delegated to the daddy doll)—and had the alligator eat up the big girl again. I asked what the mommy did then, and Becky said that the mommy cried and went away. I asked about the daddy doll, and she said he was not there. When asked if he was coming back, she said, "Yes, he's at work."

Becky reenacted the alligator approaching and gobbling up the bigger girl doll several times, getting more and more excited and violent—banging them together and throwing them about. Then, she told me the big girl was bad and that was why the alligator ate her up. I asked if the little girl was sad about the big girl getting eaten up and she said, "No, she was bad." Becky then stood up and ran over to where the puppets were and grabbed up several, seeming to become more and more excited. She said they were going to dance, but she quickly began to knock them into each other. I commented that the puppets seemed to just want to fight today, not dance. She said that they were not nice and she would have to spank them. As the end of her session was approaching, I told her that there were only a few minutes left and that she would need to finish her story and pick up the toys. I then told her she would be coming for another visit and that her mother and sister would come with her. She did not respond directly to this statement, but as she picked up each of the toys to put it away, she told me that her sister would not be allowed to play with it when she came next time. I asked if there was anything in the room her sister could play with when she came, and Becky said no.

Several hypotheses were suggested to me by Becky's play session. First, because the big sister seemed to be the bad one in the play despite the fact that Becky's mother had reported that the older sister was, if anything, almost too perfect, I hypothesized that Becky felt some strong competition with her sister for involvement with her mother. Second, I hypothesized that when Becky felt odd man out in this three-person situation, she responded by having a tantrum. Because her mother's response to the tantrum—to control her—made her feel even more the odd man out (since Julie took her mother's side), a vicious circle had developed. The more Becky felt odd man out, the more she attempted to exert control through her tantrums, and the more the mother (and her ally, Julie) attempted to control Becky, which resulted in Becky feeling even more left out.

To interrupt this process, I decided to design an intervention that would have the mother request the tantrum behavior from her daughter and put mother and daughter together by themselves (excluding the older sister). Because the mother responded to Becky's tantrums by attempting to force her to stop them, it would be quite different to have the mother foster Becky's tantrums. Thus, I decided to prescribe that the temper tantrums be executed under the mother's direction, and then monitor whether this was carried out and whether there was any change in the frequency of the tantrum behavior at school or at home.

To motivate the mother—as well as Becky—to carry out this intervention, I decided to construct and deliver a benevolent rationale. A benevolent frame was chosen because the mother had revealed a benevolent concern for Becky (mixed, of course, with some exasperation) in describing the child and the cause of her problem behavior. The following excerpt reveals how this framework was constructed and delivered to the mother.

Psychologist: Mrs. Carter, I wanted to talk with you about Becky now that I have had a chance to meet with her. You were right on the mark about Becky being affected by the changes you have had to go through.

Mother: I was afraid of that.

Psychologist: Let me tell you about some of the things that I noticed with Becky. But first let me say that the situation is by no means hopeless. I think there are some things you and I can do to help Becky change her behavior.

Mother: Oh, I'm relieved to hear that. I know something has got to be done.

Psychologist: Yes, but first let me tell you what I observed. In Becky's doll play she seemed to show that she was unsure of her place with you because of her sister. Do they seem to compete for your attention?

Mother: Well, Becky always seems to be squabbling with her sister. Julie is more laid back. Becky is always the one who seems to start things between them.

Psychologist: Do you think she is looking for a way to be involved with you separate and apart from Julie now that her dad is gone?

Mother: I don't know.

Psychologist: How does Becky behave with you when Julie is not around? Does she have tantrums then?

Mother: Well, Julie is rarely gone. She sticks pretty close to me. But when she is gone, Becky is much easier to handle now that I think of it.

Psychologist: I think that Becky is looking for a way separate from her sister to be involved with you.

Mother: That makes some sense, but I can't have her pitching a fit all the time.

Psychologist: I agree. That's not getting her what she wants anyway. I do have an idea I would like you to consider for helping Becky drop the tantrums. But it would require you to bring Becky and Julie in for us to try it out. Would you be willing to consider it?

Mother: Yes, I've got to do something.

Becky, her sister, and her mother came in three days later. During those three days, Becky had had two more outbursts at school. The account that follows describes how this session was conducted.

Becky came in with a frown on her face, appearing very different from the sunny, active little girl in the earlier play session. She stuck close to her mother, standing in front of her and leaning into her lap. She said little, while her older sister walked about the room, talking and looking at the toys. I asked if their mother had explained why they were coming, and Julie quickly piped up, saying, "We were coming to talk about Becky's bad temper." I said that I wasn't sure what Becky's temper looked like and asked Becky if she could show me what she looked like when she got mad. Before Becky had much time to answer, Julie told me that Becky had gotten really mad at her mother in the shopping mall the day before. I asked Becky to show me what she did when she got really mad, because I knew sometimes people get a little bit angry and other times it's quite loud and it looks and sounds very different. Becky didn't answer me, but pouted out her lip and cast down her eyes. She then buried her head in her mother's lap. Julie quickly jumped into the breach and asked if she could show me Becky's behavior in place of her. I turned to Becky and asked if that was OK with her. She was silent. Julie then made a little scream and stomped her foot. Becky looked sideways at her sister with her head still buried in her mother's lap. She angrily said, "That's not what I do!" I asked Becky to show me a tantrum since her sister couldn't do it right. She was silent, her head still buried in her mother's lap, but gave a small stomp of her foot. I said that it sounded like it must have made a very little noise, and asked if she usually made a bigger noise. She nodded her head. Then her sister said, "Becky even yells louder than baby Brad." "Who's he?" I asked. Becky's mother stated that he was her sister's two-year-old boy.

I complimented Becky on having a talent to make such a loud tantrum—bigger than her baby cousin, who was a boy, and even bigger than her sister, who was older. I said that she had a special talent that no other kid in her family had and that it was very important that she not lose it. I then directed that Becky should play a special game with her mother so she would not lose her ability to have a tantrum louder and stronger than anyone else in the family. To do this, Becky and her mother would have to decide on a time each day when Becky could practice having a tantrum for mother for about five minutes. This should be a time when only Becky and her mother would practice in a place by themselves. Becky's sister was not to be involved in this practice but was to busy herself with something else. I then directed Becky's mother to decide with Becky when they would practice and where. Becky's mother told her that early in the morning before school was the best time for her. Becky nodded her head. They then decided that her mother's bedroom would be the place they would practice. During all this time, Becky had her head buried in her mother's lap. I then directed the three of them to pretend it was early morning before school and they were practicing the tantrum. Becky's mother hugged her and then told her to put on a loud, angry tantrum. Becky gave a weak stab at stomping her foot and then snuggled back on her mother. When Julie started to talk, I reminded her that she was to pretend to be off playing and that this was to involve just her mother and Becky. Julie then picked up a toy and pretended to play with it while she looked out of the corner of her eye at her mother and sister.

Meanwhile, Becky's mother coaxed Becky to try a little harder to act angry and give a little scream. Becky reluctantly gave a weak little squeak and then leaned back on her mother.

I said that I knew it would be hard to pretend, but maybe it would get easier the more Becky and her mother played this. I emphasized that it would be very important for them to play this game every morning, even on mornings when Becky did not feel like it, so she would not lose her ability to have such loud tantrums. The two of them agreed to have their practice each morning for five minutes in the mother's bedroom. I pointed out that if Becky started to have a tantrum during the day, her mother was to remind her that this was not the time to practice her tantrum and that she would have to wait to practice during the tantrum practice time. I pointed out that if Becky were away from home, such as at school or a store, when she started to have a tantrum, she should be told that she would have to wait until she got home to have her tantrum at the place and time agreed. I then gave Becky's mother a simple checksheet on which she could record daily whether the practice session was carried out and if an off-time tantrum had occurred. I gave a second record sheet to the mother to give to Becky's teacher to report any off-time tantrums that occurred at school.

Becky, Julie, and their mother came in for a second session a week later. The mother reported that she had made time for the tantrum practice with Becky for five minutes each morning before school. However, Becky had only half-heartedly practiced. The mother reported that she often ended up trying to coax Becky to have a tantrum, and she and Becky frequently ended up giggling because it was something Becky seemed to goof around with. Often Becky's mother would end up tickling and hugging her. Referring to the record sheet (which I later collected), the mother also indicated that there had been only one time when Becky started to have a tantrum during the day. On that occasion Becky was reminded that it was not her practice time, and she stopped. There were no other times Becky had a tantrum outside the home, either in school or in a store. The following remarks were made in the session.

Julie: Becky wasn't bad at all. (Becky looked pleased with herself.)

Psychologist: (In response to the news that Becky had not practiced much, I expressed puzzlement and concern.) Becky, I'm really worried. I'm afraid you are not practicing enough. Maybe you will lose your touch! It is very important that you practice your tantrum making. You can't let this slide! I think you and your mom will have to practice even harder this week to make up for last week! (I then suggested to Becky and her mother that they extend their practice a minute longer each day the following week. The mother agreed to this request, but Becky looked angrily at me. I asked if she would be willing to go a minute more each day. She pouted and said nothing.)

After the mother agreed to the time increase, she spent the remainder of the session talking about her plans to lease an apartment and to change nursing jobs (she was currently on the night shift for two weeks, and then the day shift for two) so that her family's daily schedule could be a little more consistent. She also reported that she had decided to go ahead with her plans to divorce the children's father, and she had talked to Julie and Becky about her decision. As she talked, the girls played quietly with each other. Since the tantrums had not occurred at home or at school during the week, I agreed that another meeting would not be scheduled, that she and Becky would continue their early-morning practice sessions and her recordkeeping, and that a follow-up call would be made two weeks hence to see what had happened.

Three weeks later follow-up phone calls were made to the child's teacher and mother. The teacher reported that there had been no temper tantrums at school. The mother reported that Becky had had no further tantrums at home. She also stated that the morning after their last session with me, Becky had openly stated that she didn't want to practice anymore, she just wanted to play. So she and her mother had spent the few minutes they had together each morning for the next week playing together in what she called "tickle sessions." The mother stated that for the past two weeks Julie had been a part of these sessions because Becky had requested that her mother include Julie in their tickle time. The mother sent me her records for the six-week period. As she attested, there was a sharp drop in the tantrums, with none occurring after the first week.

The dramatic disappearance of the tantrum behavior that occurred in this case is not unusual. Often such symptomatic behaviors can be terminated without a single further occurrence, merely by having the behavior responded to differently. However, a careful inquiry was necessary to clearly establish the interactional elements that kept the tantrums going and to identify a frame of reference that could be used to justify the mother relinquishing her old response to the tantrums and trying a new one. Two elements in the original situation suggested a possible alternative solution. First, the mother's original response to Becky's tantrum behavior involved attempting to control Becky either by talking to her and demanding her compliance or by punishing her through spanking her. Rather than stop her tantrums, these responses served only to intensify them as Becky, feeling put down in front of a sister she was competing with, pushed even harder to get the upper hand. An alternative solution to this dilemma that interrupted the vicious circle was to have the mother prescribe that Becky carry out the tantrum behavior. This brought the tantrum behavior, which had previously been considered involuntary, under the mother's control rather than Becky's, but in a way in which the mother could respond to Becky positively rather than defensively. Expressing concern that Becky might lose her touch was a further contradiction that served to link Becky and mother together. A second element in the original situation concerned the mother's beliefs about the cause of her daughter's misbehavior. Since the mother viewed the child as troubled by the family's separation, a benevolent frame was used as the rationale for the tantrum practice sessions, which on the surface might have seemed quite outlandish.

Clearly, a major advantage of this type of intervention is that it engages the parent in the cure. The intervention was presented in such a way as to restore the mother's confidence in herself as well as to generate more positive feelings for the child as the problem behavior disappeared. For Becky, it provided a way in which she could be involved with her mother in a nonconflicting yet firm way. In addition, this case required only four hours of actual contact with the child and members of her family. This is far less time than might eventually be required in responding to the tantrums if they were allowed to remain unchecked.

CHAPTER 10

A Case of Sporadic Stealing

I first heard of Kenny D., a twelve-year-old boy, from Mrs. G., his sixth-grade homeroom teacher, six weeks into the new school year. She told me that Kenny had stolen some items from other students on two different occasions. Mrs. G. reported that the first incident had involved Kenny stealing three comic books belonging to another boy. Another student had reported seeing Kenny take the missing comics, yet when Mrs. G. confronted him regarding this, he refused to acknowledge the theft. Mrs. G. had then phoned Kenny's home to speak with his parents about this. Kenny's mother answered and became very upset when informed of her son's stealing. She attributed Kenny's behavior to his difficulty accepting changes that had occurred in the family. This explanation had made Kenny's teacher unsure whether she should punish Kenny, overlook the incident, or refer him for counseling. She finally decided to merely explain to him that since stealing made others see him as untrustworthy, and since he, of course, did not want that to happen, he was to return the stolen comics and not steal again.

A week later, however, Kenny was involved in a second stealing incident. A classmate's suspenders had been found in Kenny's locker, and he was accused of stealing them. Although Mrs. G. had taken Kenny into a separate office and confronted him about the suspenders, she reported that Kenny just sat silently. She then asked him if there was anything going on at home that made him do this. He answered no. Puzzled, Mrs. G. decided she would inform Kenny's mother about this second incident and recommend that Kenny see me for counseling.

As I listened to Kenny's teacher, it appeared that she alternated between viewing Kenny as bad and viewing him as disturbed, with her response to him shifting accordingly between lecturing and anxious inquiry as to why he misbehaved. Mrs. G.'s view that Kenny was bad seemed shaped by the fact that not only had she become exasperated trying to get him to admit his guilt in the stealing incidents, but she had also had difficulty getting him to settle down and do his written work. However, along with these feelings she appeared to believe that Kenny had problems. This view was strongly reinforced by the teacher's conversation with Kenny's mother after the first stealing incident. Consequently, when Kenny's mother was contacted about the second stealing incident, Mrs. G. encouraged her to see me as well.

Kenny's mother phoned me soon after I had spoken with the teacher. Instead of discussing Kenny's specific mishaps, however, she talked at length about her family situation, which she saw as contributing directly to Kenny's difficulties. She reported that she and Kenny's father had divorced some four years earlier, that she had custody of her two sons from that marriage (Kenny's brother was two years younger than he and was described as no problem), and that she had remarried shortly after the divorce to a man with whom Kenny did not get along. Kenny's natural father lived across the country and maintained only sporadic contact with his two sons. However, her current husband, Kenny's stepfather, was very much involved with her in raising her two sons. Mrs. D. described him as inexperienced in dealing with children and impatient in responding to them. She felt he was particularly short-tempered in dealing with Kenny, who she admitted was moody and difficult to live with. She reported having tried unsuccessfully to get Kenny to tell her what made him steal and now hoped that he might talk to me if I were to meet with him.

I asked Mrs. D. if she thought Kenny would be resistant to coming in, and she replied that she was not sure but did not know what else to do. She began to explain further about this; however, I interrupted her and told her that I felt it would be best in the long run if she and her husband came in for the first session and brought both their sons so that I might get some basic information from each of them about the situation. I then made an appointment to meet with all of them two days later. (In a child-centered problem such as this one, an adult such as a parent or teacher is often the person most concerned about the problem. Since the adult also has a great deal of power either in the family or the classroom, I usually anticipate I will be doing the majority of the work with her. Thus, having her come in with the child conveys the message that she is the one asking for my help in dealing with the child. On occasion, as in this case, I may see the child with his parents and siblings in the first interview. In general, when an adult presents a child as the problem, I do not start by seeing the child alone.)

Mr. and Mrs. D. and their two sons arrived on time. They were both potters, and the fact that they were casually dressed, though well-groomed, fit my artistic stereotype. Both of them were in their mid thirties. Their two sons, Kenny and Peter, twelve and ten, entered the room like small whirlwinds, checking out the camera and TV, then picking up chalk and scribbling on a blackboard. The boys had obviously come right from school. Because I had had some phone contact with Mrs. D. but none with Mr. D., I addressed him first as to how he saw the situation. (I wanted to assess his motivation for participating.) As Mr. D. began to speak, his words were drowned out by the noise of the two boys at the blackboard squabbling over who would get to use the one piece of chalk available. The parents seemed uncomfortable, yet made no move to structure their son's behavior. Consequently, I told the parents, "Feel free to deal with your sons here in the office as you would at home." Mr. D. responded by explaining that he and his wife had discussed how they should deal with the boys in my office and had decided to do nothing so that I could get a better picture of how they behaved. I said, "I could see how you might assume that, but, in fact, I need to hear your point of view. Unless the boys settle down, I won't be able to." I then redirected them to deal with the boys as they would at home. Mr. D. looked at Mrs. D., and she somewhat haltingly directed both boys to quiet down and take their seats. They ignored her. She then asked each boy by name to sit down and be quiet. Peter took his seat. Kenny continued to draw at the board. Mr. D. then boomed out, "Kenny, didn't you hear what your mother said? Sit down!" This transaction seemed to leave the mother harried and drained of energy and the stepfather irritated.

I then asked Mr. and Mrs. D. if this was the way it was at home with both boys squabbling and Kenny seeming to be more resistant to his mother's requests. Mr. D. said, "Yes, it's always a battle with Kenny. Peter will do what we say, but Kenny always has to be forced to do what we expect. His mother tries to reason with him, but he just ignores her. Finally, I get so mad with him running all over her, that I jump in and make him do what she says." Mrs. D. quickly broke in, "I know Kenny has had a hard time accepting Jim [Mr. D.] as his dad, and it probably doesn't help when he forces him to do what I say. But I just can't seem to get him to do what he is supposed to do. And now this stealing! This really has me worried."

I asked her if Kenny had ever stolen things from his classmates before. She looked at him and answered, "To my knowledge, no." Without my asking, she then provided information on how she had handled the stealing situations, saying, "And when I asked him why he stole these things, what was the matter—he just hung his head and wouldn't say anything." (This comment started me thinking that maybe Mrs. D. was doing too much asking and so defining her position as weak and ineffective, rather than telling her son what she expected and taking appropriate actions to ensure his compliance. However, I made no comment about this, only tucked it away for further analysis.)

I then asked Mr. D. how he had responded to the stealing situation. He said, "I asked Kenny about it. You know,
why he did it. And he told me he was set up by some of the
other kids. But I don't know whether to believe him or not."
Mrs. D. then cut in and said, "I asked Kenny if he knew it
was wrong to steal. He just answered yes." Mr. D. then said,
"Kenny has a bad habit of always laying the blame some-
where else. You know, I used to feel sorry for him. I thought
maybe he had had a lot of changes to adjust to quickly, like
Martha [Kenny's mother] says. I tried to do things with him,
but he just gave me a hard time. So I just have washed my
hands of him." Although his style of response was more definite than Mrs. D.'s, his statements about the problem were
mixed and contradictory. On the one hand, he seemed to view
Kenny as bad (spoiled, pouty, and unwilling to accept responsibility for his actions); on the other hand, his efforts to be
understanding and queries as to what was the matter reflected
a view of Kenny as disturbed (having adjustment problems).

During this time, Kenny and Peter itched about in their
seats poking at each other and periodically being told by their
mother to sit still. I turned to Kenny and asked him what he
thought was the problem. He did not reply immediately. After
only a brief moment his mother began to pressure him,
"Come on, answer Dr. A." This obviously irritated him and
made him more reluctant to talk, but finally he said, "I don't
get along with the kids at school." However, Mrs. D. continued to press him, "Now, tell her what really happened!" Soon,
mother and son were arguing: "Do I always have to do something right when you say?" "I wish I wouldn't have to tell
you what to do, Kenny." "Well, why don't you get on Peter
like you do me?" "Peter doesn't act like you do. If you
behaved yourself, I wouldn't have to treat you different!" The
pattern was plain: The boy made accusations or complaints,
and the mother responded with explanations and defensive
arguments, while the father looked on in exasperated silence.
The pattern repeated over and over during the session.

I drew the session to a close and said that I wanted to
think about what had been discussed and make my recom-

mendations to Mr. and Mrs. D. the next time we met. I asked that the two parents plan to come in without their sons for this next session. Although much of the session had seemed chaotic and emotional, I felt I was beginning to get a pretty clear idea of the problem and how it was being handled. Kenny appeared to be misbehaving at school and at home in small but persistent ways. His mother and stepfather, as well as his teacher, seemed to handle Kenny's misbehavior mainly by talk. I had heard nothing about any consequences of any note resulting from either stealing incident. All three adults seemed to flip-flop back and forth between viewing Kenny as bad and viewing him as troubled, with the latter view predominating. Even though the talking was not getting results, all three adults seemed to be persisting in believing that communication was the answer—Kenny just needed to talk to them and tell them why he did what he did. Mrs. D. in particular seemed to play a pivotal role in maintaining the view that Kenny was troubled. For example, even when acknowledging that Kenny had not followed her command to move to his seat, she linked it with his nonacceptance of her new husband. Although there may have been some truth to her perception that Kenny and her husband did not get along, to me Kenny seemed to act more as though he did not want to obey her rather than as though he were troubled. In thinking about how she allowed this view of Kenny to predominate, I wondered whether she felt some guilt over putting her children through a divorce and consequently thought they needed to be dealt with gently. I wondered further if her new husband's critical response to Kenny triggered her to act in an even more protective manner toward her son.

Preparing for my second session with Mr. and Mrs. D., I reviewed how I had seen them interact with Kenny. First, Mrs. D. and, to a lesser extent, Mr. D. appeared to view Kenny as disturbed by the mother's divorce and remarriage more than bad. Thus, his stealing at school and his resistance at home appeared to be attributed to his lack of adjustment to his parents' divorce. Because Mrs. D. viewed Kenny as troubled, she seemed to feel he needed to be treated fragilely and so either softened her demands or stated them indirectly. Second, Mr. and Mrs. D. often became involved in defensive arguments with Kenny that were unproductive and only served to give him an authority he did not need or deserve. If Mr. and Mrs. D. could instead tell Kenny what he was to do without getting involved in defensive arguments, Kenny would be faced with explicit commands to which he would be forced to respond more explicitly (that is, without playing hard-of-hearing or trying to sidetrack his parents).

I figured, however, that several steps would be necessary to disengage Mr. and Mrs. D. from their previous responses. First, they would have to be willing to involve themselves in the change effort rather than see Kenny as getting fixed by someone else. Second, because Mrs. D. in particular seemed to flip-flop in her attitude toward Kenny when he disobeyed her, she would have to be motivated to be more direct with him. For her to do that, it would be necessary for her to move away from feeling responsible for making him troubled. Finally, a specific target area for such a change would have to be located.

I decided that the major goals of my conference with Mr. and Mrs. D. would be to involve them more centrally in the change effort and to motivate Mrs. D. to follow my suggestions on how to deal with Kenny differently. When Mr. and Mrs. D. arrived, they were quite upset. They reported that Kenny had gone to a store on the way home from school the day of our meeting, stolen a toy, and then been discovered playing with it outside the house by his mother. Having deduced that Kenny had stolen the toy, Mrs. D. had attempted to talk with him about why he had done this. Kenny, however, had refused to talk. Mr. and Mrs. D. then disagreed on why Kenny had done this, and consequently on what to do about it. Mr. D. felt that Kenny consciously stole the toy because he wanted to play with it, while Mrs. D. seemed to think Kenny's theft might be a sign he was troubled and upset.

I decided to emphasize the seriousness and difficult nature of the situation: "Clearly, while most children lust after and may take an item belonging to another child, to steal something a second and now a third time indicates that Kenny has not gotten the message of what you expect from him in the way of honest behavior. This is a serious problem, and you are very correct to be worried." (Since Mrs. D. in particular had said this, I assumed she would agree strongly with my statement, which proved correct.) I next asked them how they were handling the latest stealing incident. Mr. D. said very forcefully that he thought they should punish Kenny. Mrs. D.'s answer was more confused and rambling. She talked of needing to teach him not to steal, of feeling like he did this because he was upset, and of having difficulty knowing just what was on Kenny's mind. Mrs. D. seemed to feel that Mr. D.'s response was not the correct one, yet she did not appear to have a definite alternative in mind. This disagreement had led to their taking no action on the incident. I wondered if this was a typical way in which a clear response to Kenny got bogged down—with Mr. D. taking a stern position and Mrs. D. sabotaging Mr. D.'s position. I decided to attempt to shift them to thinking in terms of taking some action by asking, "So you obviously think there's an important lesson here for Kenny to learn?" Mrs. D. agreed, and I went on to suggest that Kenny needed to learn exactly what his parents would do if he stole, and that this could be done by their deciding how to handle this stealing incident. I then asked them, "What do you want to have happen?"

Mrs. D. looked at Mr. D. at that point. To block Mrs. D. from trying to turn it over to either Mr. D. or me to handle, I said, "You know, in hearing about this incident, I realize that Kenny has gone out of his way to have you, Mrs. D., be the one to catch him. It is clear that you are the one of greatest importance to Kenny. I know that Mr. D. tries to offer his ideas, but it seems that Kenny considers you the one with the most influence. However, even though you are really the only one in a position to help Kenny, I can certainly understand how you would like to just wash your hands of him and hope someone else might deal with him. After all, he sounds like he can be a hard person to get along with." As I hoped,

Mrs. D. said, "No, I don't want to do that. I'm worried about him, but I don't want to give up on him. But I just don't know how to get through to him that he should not steal." I suggested that our time could be spent talking about how they might want to teach him this.

Then, in order to get more information on Mrs. D.'s own views as well as those of her husband, I asked her, "What is your best guess as to the reason that Kenny is having these stealing problems?" Mrs. D. said she worried that because her divorce from Kenny's father had been a turbulent one, and because Mr. D. and Kenny had locked horns a lot over Kenny doing what Mr. D. told him to do, she was worried that her involvement with another man was having a bad impact on Kenny. She was afraid he was angry at her for what she had put him through and so was doing something really wrong so that she would pay attention to him. Almost at once, though, she shifted and said, "But then I wonder if Kenny just needs some discipline."

Since this last comment was in line with my own thinking, I picked up on it right away. "It sounds like Kenny does need you to tell him flat out what you expect from him, without any discussion or reasoning." However, since I had a hunch that Mrs. D. was feeling very guilty toward Kenny, and that this got in the way of taking effective measures to handle him, I followed up with, "But I don't expect you will do this. You know, Mrs. D., you seem very frustrated by his behavior. But you seem unable to correct him because you blame yourself for his problem. You seem to believe that if you had not divorced or had not remarried, Kenny would not behave this way."

Mrs. D. started to cry, and nodded her head in agreement. She said, "I just had to get out of my marriage to Kenny's dad. It was eating me alive. But I don't want Kenny or Peter to suffer for it." This statement confirmed my hunch that Mrs. D. was feeling very guilty toward Kenny and that this got in the way of effectively setting limits with him. I knew I needed to deal with this before anything else could be done. To do this, I said, "You know, the most important thing here is not the past, but where we go from here." She agreed, and I went on to say, "However, the past is important because it keeps getting in the way because it is unsettled, especially with regard to your responsibility for Kenny's problems. You know, you may be taking on too much of the responsibility for Kenny and his problems. Jim here, and your first husband, and the people at school, and even Kenny himself may also be partly responsible for these problems. However, since I don't see any way to judge reliably just how much blame and responsibility belongs to you versus each of them, and to get this over with, let's suppose we do like judges and lawyers in court do and say that this is all your fault." This tactic of exaggerating the mother's position of feeling guilty about Kenny paralleled a tactic reported by John Weakland in a case entitled "OK—So You've Been a Bad Mother" (Weakland, 1977b).

Mrs. D. nodded, but with a half-smile, and then looked at her husband. Next, I said, "OK, since that is now settled, you are the crucial one if Kenny is to change. You are the one Kenny looks to. While Jim can help you implement whatever you decide, he needs to follow your lead, and do whatever you decide to do with Kenny." Mrs. D. nodded her head.

She then asked, "But how do you get through to a kid like Kenny?" To me, this signaled a small but important shift away from looking only at the why of Kenny's behavior. This was confirmed when she went on to state, "Kenny needs to know that we won't tolerate him stealing. He needs to go back to the store and tell the manager he stole the toy and give him the money for it. He has some money he's been saving up. He'll have to use that to pay for this toy he stole." I replied, "That sounds really clear to me, what you expect him to do. That lets him know exactly what he needs to learn about how you will respond to his stealing. But I wonder if you will really be able to do this. Kenny knows just how to push your buttons—especially your guilt button—and get you involved explaining to him and convincing him. So you say you'll tell him, but I'll be ready to say 'I told you so' when you don't do it."

We set up another appointment, and then I said to Mr. and Mrs. D., "You know, it might be important not to do anything too different with Kenny like telling him straight out what you expect of him. After all, he's been quite used to you being very patient and understanding with him. Maybe you could just imagine in your mind how in the thick of battle with him you might just say flat out what you want him to do. But don't do it, it might be too much of a change for him. You might, however, make a mental note when a battle is raging of how you might tell him what you expect. But, of course, don't do it right now. It might be too much of a change for him."

These instructions were given to encourage them to become more direct in their requests of Kenny. While these instructions seemed to put some restraint on implementing a different response with Kenny, in reality they were designed to decrease the possibility that they would be rejected by Mr. and Mrs. D.

When Mr. and Mrs. D. returned a week later, they reported that it had not been an easy week. In contrast to my parting instructions to make no change, they had agreed to follow through on what Mrs. D. had talked about doing concerning Kenny's theft. Mrs. D. had made him take part of his savings, accompany her, apologize to the store manager, and pay for the stolen toy. Kenny had "yelled and swore up and down," but Mrs. D. had made him carry out these steps. The next day, Kenny had failed to come straight home after school and was unaccounted for for about three hours. Both Mr. and Mrs. D. had gone out searching for him. Mrs. D. had located him sitting in the woods close to their home within easy earshot of their many calls to him. She reported being sick with worry about him and then getting really angry when she discovered he was within earshot of the house. She said, "I just got to boiling at the thought of his making us work so hard to find him." Apparently this incident had convinced her that he was acting up (rather than acting troubled) and thus needed some limits set. She said further, "I was so mad at him, I didn't say anything; I just told him to go to his room. He wanted to come out later, but I said he was to stay there." During the time she spoke, Mr. D. nodded his head in agreement, and then said, "I think both of us were ready to kill him at that point. But Martha stuck to her guns and made him stay in his room all night."

This report convinced me that Mrs. D., in particular, was moving toward less talk, less anxiety, less defensiveness, and more effective action with Kenny. But not completely, however. She said, "But it's still such a struggle getting him to do his work around the house. What can we do about that?" I answered, "Well, let's take this one step at a time. You know, it seems that when you want him to do something and just say simply, 'I'd like you to do such and such'— without much discussion or argument—that things go a lot more smoothly. So simply tell him what you want him to do, and when you get his typical negative reaction say, 'I can't make you do it. If you don't, I don't know what I'll do about it.'" Mr. and Mrs. D. looked at each other and nodded in agreement. Mr. D. said, "You know, that might be a good way to handle Kenny because it will throw him off. He won't be expecting that." Both Mr. and Mrs. D. then agreed to try this and to keep a record describing each incident, their response, and Kenny's subsequent reaction.

I then suggested they consider how Kenny might get them sidetracked from responding so casually and push them into arguing with him. "It seems like Kenny really knows how to push your buttons to get you mad at him so that you get hooked into convincing him of what he needs to do. How do you think he'll do this when you try this response of saying, 'I'd like you to do such and such, but I can't make you do it'?" Mr. D. said, "He usually just acts like he hasn't heard what I've said." Mrs. D. agreed. "So that really gets your goat and sets you off to explaining and haranguing?" I asked. "Yes," said Mr. D. I retorted, "I can imagine it will be very hard not to let him get you involved in explaining to him or scolding him. We'll have to see who is stronger, won't we?" With that I turned to setting up another appointment with them a week later.

When Mr. and Mrs. D. came in, they seemed in good spirits. I immediately said, "I get to score a point for Kenny, don't I?" They laughed, and Mrs. D. replied, "No, actually he's been pretty good. But we've kind of backed off some too with him. I mean, both Jim and I have just told him what he was to do this week, not made a big furor about it or nagged him." I said, "Gee, do you think he's kind of biding his time, waiting to see if you really mean this?" Mrs. D. said, "Well, he's been doing what we said, but we are kind of nervous, wondering if this is going to last. Of course, he hasn't been perfect. He and Peter still went at it every once in a while. But he wasn't so nasty like he's been." Again I felt that both Mr. and Mrs. D. were making considerable progress in changing how they were responding to Kenny, and I wanted to consolidate this not by reassuring them but by challenging their resolve. Thus I asked, "What do you think he might do to really make you slip back to what you were doing before, doing a lot of explaining and arguing to get him to do what you say?" Mrs. D. mentioned that they had had no negative reports from school in the past two weeks, but indicated that if he stole again, she might slip back into haranguing him.

By this point, Mr. and Mrs. D. were indicating some positive changes and increased confidence in how they were responding to Kenny. However, rather than shift to a stance of optimism and congratulations, which might set them up for a discouraging letdown as soon as they encountered a difficult situation—which was bound to occur—I kept on the same track of pointing out that they would meet further difficulties, but there were ways they could handle them. They indicated that they felt they no longer needed to meet with me. I said—still maintaining my doubting and pessimistic stance—that if they had any more tests to face with Kenny, I wasn't sure they would pass them, but they knew where they could call me if they did not.

I did not receive any more negative reports about Kenny from Mrs. G., Kenny's teacher. Four weeks after ending with the D. family I mailed Kenny's teacher a follow-up questionnaire in which I asked whether Kenny's behavior had

changed. She completed it and mailed it back to me, reporting that there had been no more stealing incidents at school
and that Kenny was doing his classwork without her constant
reminders. Since there were no further phone calls from the
D.'s, approximately six weeks after our last meeting I called
them to ask how things were going. Mrs. D. said there had
been some ups and downs, but generally things were much
better. She indicated that both she and Mr. D. remembered to
use some of the things we'd talked about, the main one being
not to nag Kenny so much but just tell him what to do. I said
that it is often hard to know when to stop explaining, she
agreed and thanked me for calling, and as I hung up I felt
that some significant change had been started through our
four sessions together.

       As can be seen, it is often adults who can most effec-
tively help students to change. Adults are often more committed than students to changing in the problem situation, so
involving them can bring about excellent results in relatively
short periods of time.

CHAPTER 11

A Case of
Refusal to Attend School

by Patricia Carrow

This case was selected for inclusion in this book for two reasons. First, it deals with a situation confronted by many school helping professionals—the student who refuses to attend school. Second, it illustrates how brief strategic intervention can be successfully used in situations defined as crises by those involved.

School counselors and other staff members are often confronted with unexpected crisis situations during a school day. Although students may seek out a counselor on their own when a crisis occurs, frequently it is a parent, a teacher, or another school staff member who brings a student perceived as in crisis to the attention of the counselor. When this occurs, the counselor often finds that the problem behaviors underlying the current crisis are embedded and of long duration. Usually the methods that have been applied to resolve the problem behavior have been ineffective, and others involved with the problem are frustrated and angry at their failure to get the student on the right track. Because of this failure, the student is brought to the counselor for help. Unfortunately, as a rule more of the same solution that has already proven ineffective is expected to be applied. In the following case, a parent and school staff person have contacted the school's counselor after their efforts to get a fifteen-year-old girl named Lisa to attend school have failed.

The first few weeks of a new school year are always

179

hectic ones for school practitioners. In addition to helping students cope with various personal problems, a school counselor is usually involved in greeting, registering, and orienting students and responding to students dissatisfied with course assignments. It was on just such an average day that Lisa was brought to my office by Mr. Parsons, a businesslike and determined dean of students, and Mrs. R., Lisa's mother. Mr. Parsons interrupted my conversation with a student to say, "Mrs. C., I'd like to see you about a student. Her mother is here, and we'd like to take care of this problem so that she can get back to work." I took a few minutes to finish up with the student and invited them in.

As the three of them entered my office, I greeted them with a smile, directed them to sit where they liked, and made a few quick observations. Mr. Parsons seemed very much in charge. He directed Lisa and her mother to sit down and then quickly launched into his description of the problem. Mrs. R., Lisa's mother, looked teary-eyed and anxious. As she listened to Mr. Parsons's account, she nodded her head in agreement. Lisa, a slim blond girl of fifteen, sat with her back against the wall. She was silent as she listened to the adults around her describe her troublesome behavior, motives, and bleak future to me—the person charged with helping her. She sat motionless, showed no visible reaction to what was said, and stared at the floor. Lisa did not acknowledge or respond to any of the accusations or admonitions directed at her by Mr. Parsons or her mother. She retained her silence, seemingly her only line of defense.

Because I have found it important to be cautious about following along with what is expected of me in solving a student problem, I listened carefully to what was being said by Mr. Parsons and Mrs. R. I wanted to observe the reactions each had to the other's views of the problem and how it should be resolved. Rather than commit myself to their ideas, I needed to assess whether Mr. Parsons's and Lisa's mother's very efforts to get Lisa to attend school might actually be provoking her nonattendance.

Mr. Parsons related the incidents that had brought them

to my office that morning. During this account, Mrs. R. inter-mittently mumbled agreement and expressed her frustration and concern.

Mr. Parsons: It seems Lisa here has been cutting school on a daily basis. Her mother is terribly worried and upset. She says she can't do a thing with her, and she refuses to go to school. She's talked to Lisa and told her she has to go to school, that it's important that she get an education. I've talked to Lisa too. I've told her she has to attend school. That's the law. I've asked Lisa why she doesn't want to go to school, but she refuses to talk to me or to her mother. If we knew what the problem was, the reason she won't come to school, we could help her. But she just won't tell us. (He turns to Lisa.) Lisa, you have your whole family upset about this. Your mom is upset and worried about you. She can't go to work. You have younger brothers and sisters who look up to you. We want to help you, but we can't if you don't tell us what the problem is.

Lisa: (Sits silently, staring at the floor.)

Counselor: Mrs. R., it seems that you and a lot of people are worried and concerned about Lisa cutting school. And you're really confused and frustrated because she isn't telling you why she's not going. You want to help her, but you don't know how.

Mother: I've tried to talk to her but she acts just like she's doing now, she stares at the floor and doesn't say a word. I don't know what to do with her. (She shakes her head and cries softly.) Lisa, please tell us what's wrong! (Lisa responds only with silence.) You know you have to get an education. Mr. Parsons says it's the law and that I might have to go to court if I can't get you to go to school. (She sobs as her pleas are greeted with more silence and turns to me.) What can I do? She won't listen to me!

As Mr. Parsons and Lisa's mother told their story, I wanted to be careful not to focus my questions and comments on Lisa. Their conversation centered on Lisa's behavior and its negative effect on her mother and the family and on the deleterious effects of Lisa not getting an education. It seemed to me that this barrage was designed to pressure Lisa to cooperate and be a good girl. However, it was having just the opposite effect. She seemed to respond to these comments in the only way she knew, by being silent.

Counselor: Mrs. R., you care about what's going to happen to Lisa, and you've tried everything you can think of to help your daughter, and it's not working.

Mother: Yes, I have. I just can't get through to her.

Mr. Parsons: Lisa, do you see how upset your mother is about this? She's worried sick about you. Tell us what's wrong. We can't help you if you don't tell us how. Maybe you'll talk to Mrs. C. She's a counselor and can help you. That's why we brought you here.

The conversation continued along these same lines for another five or ten minutes, with Mr. Parsons alternately berating Lisa for upsetting everyone with her obstinate behavior and pleading with her to talk about her reasons for not going to school so that she could be helped. During this time Lisa's mother, Mrs. R., sobbed and wrung her hands and flip-flopped between telling Lisa she couldn't understand why she was doing this to her and pleading with her to talk.

As this pattern continued, it became increasingly apparent to me that alternately pleading with and haranguing Lisa was not working. She still refused to talk. Staying with this ineffective solution was only further frustrating and angering Mr. Parsons and Lisa's mother. A vicious circle was operating. Mr. Parsons and Mrs. R. had invited me to join them in this solution to the problem. They hoped that by presenting a united front of three adults, they could convince Lisa to talk about what was wrong. The harder they tried, however, the more Lisa appeared to dig in her heels and be silent. I could see that this solution would not work no matter how long we sat in my office and applied it.

Approximately forty-five minutes had elapsed when Mr. Parsons turned to me and said, "Maybe you can get through to Lisa where we have failed. Maybe you can get her to tell you why she won't come to school." Mr. Parsons assumed that I would somehow have the right words to convince Lisa to talk to us and mend her ways. This type of request to join in can be very tempting. However, instead of deciding to become part of the pattern I saw before me, I decided to take a different tack. It seemed to me that Lisa needed to be taken off the spot. The problem was how? The focus was on Lisa and her obstinate behavior. Changing the focus to put the choice of what Lisa would do about school in Lisa's hands seemed a good place to start. However, it was important to legitimize the two adults' concerns about Lisa.

I decided to start by addressing Lisa directly: "Lisa, a lot of people seem to be very worried about you. They don't know what to do to get you to talk about this situation and tell them what you want to do." I paused to see if she would respond to this. She did not—just as she had not responded to the others. I continued, "I've been watching you think about what everyone has said to you about the importance of going to school and how they are concerned about you. It seems to me that you don't want to talk about this until you have had time to think very carefully about how you want to handle it. I agree. This is important to you. You need to take the proper amount of time to think about it. To talk about it before you have thought it through might not be the best thing you could do at this point. What do you think?" (Lisa looked up for the first time and nodded.) I then turned to Lisa's mother.

Counselor: Mrs. R., I know that you really care about Lisa and want very much to help her, but right now I'm more concerned about you. You mentioned that you've had to take time off from work because of this and that your pay is docked. You've also said that you really need this job, and you're afraid if you take any more time off you may lose it.

Mrs. R.: Yes, I have to work to support my family. I can't afford to lose this job. I don't know what I'm going to do.

Lisa just keeps me upset all the time because of this school thing.

Counselor: Yes, I can see how important it is to you to take care of your family, Mrs. R., and I agree with you. You do need to take care of yourself and do what you can to keep your job. Leaving work to come down to school all the time is not helping you at work. (Mrs. R. nods in agreement.) I think Lisa needs to think very carefully about all this, and we shouldn't rush her. I also believe that it's important to you to get back to your job and do what you have to do to take care of your family. (She nods in agreement.) I have a suggestion. Since you have important business to attend to and Lisa needs some time to think without interruption, I'm willing to let her stay in the guidance office for as long as she needs. You can go to work knowing where she is and what she's doing, and she can have the time she needs to think.

Mrs. R.:   Well, I really do need to get back to work, and I'll at least know where Lisa is. OK, but what will you do with Lisa?

Counselor: Nothing. I don't think she needs me to do anything but give her the time to think things through. When she's decided what she wants to do about this situation, I'm confident she'll let us know. Lisa, is this satisfactory with you? (Lisa nods her agreement.) Mr. Parsons?

Mr. Parsons: Whatever you think. I certainly can't get her to talk. I've got some other cases I have to attend to today. I'll check with you later about Lisa.

Counselor: Fine. Lisa, you can use the guidance office for as long as you need. If you have to use the restroom, just let the secretary know. At lunchtime you can eat in the cafeteria or bring your lunch back here to eat. I'll stop by to see how you are doing throughout the day.

Mrs. R. and Mr. Parsons went their separate ways, Lisa found a comfortable chair in the guidance office, and I went to my next appointment. I knew it was critical to follow through on what I had told Lisa about having the time and place for her to think. It was not yet midmorning, and there were numerous other duties to perform. Students were coming in to drop or add a class or to talk about difficulties they were having in getting along with a teacher or another student. Teachers stopped in to talk about students they thought might not be suited for their classes. And, occasionally, a parent would phone with a concern about her child's adjustment to school or placement in a particular class. Periodically, every hour and a half, I stopped by Lisa's chair and smiled at her, asked how she was getting along, and nothing more. She would respond to my query with a shy little smile but still would not speak.

It was ten minutes until the end of the school day. Lisa had remained silent the entire time. I went over and sat next to her and said, "Lisa, it's almost time to go home. I'm wondering if you need more time to think? If you do, you may use this office again tomorrow." Still no response, but a nod and a shy smile. I walked back to my office, marveling at the strength of Lisa's resistance and wondering how long she would need before she could trust me enough to say more than a few words. The bell rang signaling the end of the day. Lisa appeared in my office doorway. She stood waiting until she got my attention. She said shyly, "I've decided what I want to do." "Fine," I said. "Tell me about it." "I've decided to come to school. But can I come here first in the morning?" "Sure," I answered, "I'll see you in the morning before classes begin." I deliberately tried to treat Lisa as though she were just another young adult who had told me she had made a decision. I accepted what she had to say without telling her what a wonderful or grown-up choice she had made or complimenting her for finally speaking. I had long ago learned that one rule of thumb that never changes in working with adolescents is not to patronize them. I've found that by following this rule I can be seen as an adult who treats them differently and listens to what they have to say.

The day had ended on an encouraging note. I felt pleased that Lisa had decided to speak to me and to attend school. Her request to come into my office in the morning created another opportunity for me to develop a relationship with her on her terms.

The next step I took with Lisa was to continue to build on our relationship. She appeared in my office the next morning about ten minutes before classes were to begin. She stood in the doorway and gave a shy smile, but did not speak. I greeted her warmly, smiling back, and asked her to come in and sit for a few moments. I began a conversation with her, trying to ask questions that focused on her opinions rather than any "why" questions.

Counselor: Lisa, you're pretty new to our school, aren't you? (She nodded.) Tell me what you think about being in ninth grade in our school.

Lisa: It's OK, I guess. I don't know too many people here. Most of the kids I went to middle school with went to the other high schools.

Counselor: You miss some of your friends very much?

Lisa: Yeah, it's not too bad when I'm in class because I'm doing stuff. I really hate study hall, though. There's nothing to do, and everybody sits next to their friends. Do I have to go there?

Counselor: Study hall sounds like a place you don't like to go to. I guess it can make you feel pretty lonely and left out when you see the other kids laughing and having a good time with their friends?

Lisa: Yeah, I wish there was some place else I could go to. Do you think I could come down here during study hall?

Counselor: That's certainly a possibility, Lisa. But I'd feel uncomfortable with having you just come here and sit for a whole class period.

Lisa: Maybe I could do something like filing or something. I want to be a secretary when I finish school.

Counselor: I could use some help. You'd have to do some things besides filing. I might want you to deliver messages to teachers in other parts of the building, or maybe show a new student around. Do you think you would be interested in doing that?

Lisa: Yeah, can I start today?

The smile on Lisa's face confirmed her excitement about doing something she felt was special. She had apparently been reluctant to attend a school where she had few, if any, friends and felt unimportant and overlooked. It seemed to me that this solution provided her with an opportunity to temporarily escape an unpleasant situation, study hall, and replace it with opportunities to feel important and useful, as well as to learn her way around the building, meet teachers, and even help new students who were as frightened as she was.

The day that Mr. Parsons and Lisa's mother brought her into my office was a turning point for Lisa. She and her family were certainly in crisis and did not know what to do. The usual pleading only led to more silence on Lisa's part as her preferred way to deal with stress or pressure from others. If the pattern of trying harder to convince Lisa to change her ways had been continued (that is, if I had joined in), Lisa might still be sitting quietly and silently rebelling by skipping school. The crisis would have continued, and Lisa would have become a problem student in the eyes of her family and the school system. I was able to keep an accurate record of Lisa's attendance and found that not only did Lisa begin to attend school regularly, she missed only a few days that year. She continued to help me in the guidance office during the fall semester. In a follow-up phone call to Lisa's mother to inform her about Lisa's progress at school, I discovered that she was a single parent with four children, with Lisa being the oldest. Lisa was seen as responsible and helpful to her mother, but always quiet. Her usual method of responding to something she did not want to do was to fall silent. In my phone conversation I reported Lisa's strengths and her silent determination to her mother. Mrs. R. seemed proud of Lisa's progress. There were no other phone calls to Mrs. R. the remainder of the year. She did not need to be called into school again because of her daughter's behavior. A crisis situation had been dealt with effectively and briefly within the context of the school.

This case shows how a commonly occurring crisis situation—a student's refusal to attend school—can be dealt with effectively and briefly in the school. While each case of school refusal has its own distinctive context and solution (what worked for Lisa would not necessarily work for another student in a similar situation), the approach to this behavior illustrated in this chapter is applicable in a wide variety of contexts.

CHAPTER 12

Brief Strategic Intervention: Using the Approach Responsibly

The ideas and techniques presented in this book are quite powerful. This does not mean, however, that they will be useful to everyone or in every situation. School helping professionals differ, as do student problem situations. No approach will always succeed or fit all users. In closing, let us consider the reasons why this approach may have mixed appeal.

What is offered here is a different option for working to resolve problems students experience in school. It is intended to increase one's options, not reduce them. I assume that most practitioners reading this book already have a number of different ways they currently respond to students experiencing problems at school. These current methods may be quite satisfactory. If so, it is pointless to try something else. Even if one feels she needs something else, this may not be the approach preferred. A number of common reactions to this approach may contribute to this feeling. These are: being discomfited by the deliberate use of therapeutic power or influence, being unsure how client confidentiality is protected, being uncomfortable with the selective disclosure implicit in reframing, and being concerned about the limits of tolerable distress encouraged in these interventions.

For school helping professionals accustomed to a more reflective model of intervention, brief strategic intervention may seem inordinately directive and controlling. Although the practitioner's authority is endorsed in most reflective or insight-oriented approaches, it is usually done at an implicit level (O'Shea and Jessee, 1982). For example, the school practitioner choosing to work with a child in play therapy, or to consult with a teacher or parent in redirecting their response to a problematic situation, is expected to decide whether an intervention is warranted and how to structure that intervention. By contrast, the practitioner's active concentration on considering his position relative to a client, which is characteristic of brief strategic intervention, may appear much more manipulative.

Issues of confidentiality and information sharing may also be confusing. Unlike individually oriented treatment approaches in which the child is the client whose confidences are to be respected, in this approach the therapeutic contract may involve several different parties (for example, school staff, family members, and the student). What implication does that have for information sharing? Many systems therapists consider the ability to control the flow of information among the parties involved a key tool for changing the interactional pattern around a problem behavior. For example, Haley (1976) advises practitioners to carefully consider their therapeutic goals when deciding how information is to be shared among those involved. He believes that information sharing should be deliberate, because restricting information creates or maintains boundaries between people, while sharing information weakens or removes boundaries.

Nowhere is this more evident than in the selective disclosure of certain information to build a rationale for a particular action directive. This reframing highlights some facts and ignores, deemphasizes, or avoids others. Some may consider this a deliberate distortion of information. However, most systems therapists contend that the practice is an ethically responsible one, and, as O'Shea and Jessee (1982) state, the ethical issue involved "is the question of whether, in so acting, the helping professional is deceiving or harming the client" (1982, p. 100). Other therapists (for example, Fisher, Anderson, and Jones, 1981) contend that when such reframing is effective it is precisely because it is truthful, that is, it accurately embodies the client's experience.

A final concern is the degree of short-term distress or risk of harm engendered by a particular intervention. For example, prescribing a problematic behavior (as in the case of Niki, the little girl who vomited at school) goes against our notions of stabilizing problematic behavior. How can escalating a problem be seen as a helpful intervention? Clearly this requires a careful determination that less disruptive change efforts have failed, that the risk of a negative outcome is small, and that the current pattern is worse than the cure.

Particularly necessary is responsible deliberation as to when these intervention methods are appropriate. Because they are potent tools, they cannot be engaged in haphazardly without a serious commitment to assess the elements of the problem situation and follow through in monitoring the change effort. The practitioner must be willing to commit time to gathering information about the problem/solution cycle, thinking through a solution shift, and motivating those involved to act differently. An intervention applied formulaically without such careful planning can lead to harm, either causing people to lose confidence and drop out of counseling or causing more severe crises. Although this book has attempted to describe a few of the guidelines to consider in selecting and developing such interventions, this is not an attempt to suggest a strict formula for designing specific interventions for specific symptoms. Each student case must be approached as unique.

Moreover, as stated in Chapter Three, this approach is ill-advised for certain types of student problem situations. For example, this approach is not applicable when dealing with a student responding to a chaotic situation either at home or at school. The structure of such situations is so loose and variable that it is often difficult to find a concrete problem/solution cycle to work on. In such situations, it is often more important to establish some kind of stability in interpersonal relationship structures than to eliminate a troublesome problem behavior in the individual.

In addition, brief strategic intervention is not appropriate in situations of acute emotional crisis. In such situations, the student and others involved with her often need a sense of cohesiveness and nurturance. Furthermore, whenever there is the potential for sharp escalation of symptomatic behaviors with strong negative consequences (for example, when severe depressive or aggressive behaviors are demonstrated), careful judgments must be made concerning the risk of using brief strategic tactics.

In conclusion, as is true with any intervention strategy, brief strategic intervention is not the answer to all school-related problems. However, when the cautions described above are kept in mind and interventions are carefully tailored to the circumstances, these intervention methods have several advantages for use in the schools. First, such intervention methods can induce quick problem resolution, which frees the student to get on with the business of learning. Second, these intervention methods allow members of the school staff to influence the student by cooperating with him rather than engendering resistance. More often than not, when a student's problem behavior cannot be changed by the school staff, it places the student (and sometimes his parents) in a one-up position relative to the staff and creates the illusion that he is in control. This one-up position is maintained when the student's behavior elicits feelings of anger, anxiety, helplessness, or exasperation in the school staff. When a brief strategic intervention is effective, the staff members have engineered an experience in which the student changes his behavior in response to their change in behavior. These changes evoke a sense of increased power in both staff and student, the sign that everybody wins. Third, by means of these methods, the school rather than the home can take the initiative for changing problematic student behavior. In those situations where a student's problem behavior is being responded to similarly at school and at home, it may be easier for the practitioner to get at the school staff's solution efforts than at the parents'. Consequently, implementation of this mode of intervention does not depend on having the cooperation of the student's family. Fourth, using brief strategic intervention methods can broaden a school staff's repertoire of behaviors so that the next time a staff member finds herself in a similar situation, she may remember the "less of the same" lesson. Finally, because it involves all the people whose responses support a student problem, brief strategic intervention allows the problem-bearer to feel more normal and less bad or incompetent. Thus, rather than place the site of pathology inside the child or his family, this intervention approach assumes the problem is merely a bad match between solution and situation.

The fact that the methods described in this book are powerful and need to be respected and handled responsibly does not mean they need to be feared, however. It is important to remember that all of the interactions one engages in with students, their parents, and school staff are powerful, whether one wishes to acknowledge that power or not. Hopefully, the practitioner will find the approach described here helpful in day-to-day interactions in school. Of course, learning any new skill takes practice. The practitioner should not set her sights too high too soon, but instead allow herself to go slowly, choosing what she may wish to try without undue pressure. If she finds that she is pushing herself to master this and is becoming discouraged, it is a good idea to let up for a while. Learning how to be helpful to others is a lifetime process, something each practitioner does at her own pace and in her own style.

REFERENCES

Amatea, E. "Brief Systemic Intervention: A Case of Temper Tantrums." *Psychology in the Schools,* 1988a, *25,* 174-183.

Amatea, E. "Engaging the Reluctant Client: Some New Strategies for the School Counselor." *The School Counselor,* 1988b, *36,* 34-40.

Amatea, E., and Lockhausen, L. "Brief Strategic Intervention: A New Approach to School Counseling Practice." *Elementary School Guidance and Counseling Journal,* 1988, *22,* 353-456.

Amatea, E., and Sherrard, P. A. "Reversing the School's Response: A New Approach to Resolving Persistent School Problems." *American Journal of Family Therapy,* 1989, *17,* 15-26.

Anderson, H., Goolishan, H., and Windermand, L. "Problem-Determined Systems: Toward Transformation in Family Therapy." *Journal of Strategic and Systemic Therapies,* 1987, *5,* 1-13.

Barlow, D., Hayes, S., and Nelson, R. *The Scientist Practitioner: Research and Accountability in Clinical and Educational Settings.* New York: Pergamon Press, 1984.

Bodin, A. "The Interactional View: Family Therapy Approaches of the M.R.I." In A. Gurman and D. Kniskern (eds.), *Handbook of Family Therapy.* In A. Gurman and D. Kniskern (eds.), *Handbook of Family Therapy.* New York: Brunner/Mazel, 1981.

Bowen, M. *Family Therapy in Clinical Practice.* New York: Jason Aronson, 1978.

DeShazer, S. *Brief Family Therapy: An Ecosystemic Approach.* New York: Guilford, 1982.

Erickson, M., and Rossi, E. *Hypnotherapy: An Exploratory Casebook.* New York: Irvington, 1979.

Fisch, R. "Sometimes It's Better for the Right Hand Not to Know What the Left Hand Is Doing." In P. Papp (ed.), *Family Therapy Full Length Case Studies.* New York: Gardner, 1977.

Fisch, R., Weakland, J. H., and Segal, L. *The Tactics of Change: Doing Therapy Briefly.* San Francisco: Jossey-Bass, 1982.

Fisher, L., Anderson, A., and Jones, J. "Types of Paradoxical Interventions and Indications and Contraindications for Use in Clinical Practice." *Family Process,* 1981, *20,* 25–35.

Haley, J. *Uncommon Therapy: The Psychiatric Techniques of Milton H. Erickson, M.D.* New York: Norton, 1973.

Haley, J. *Problem-Solving Therapy.* San Francisco: Jossey-Bass, 1976.

Haley, J. *Ordeal Therapy.* San Francisco: Jossey-Bass, 1984.

Haley, J. *Conversations with Milton H. Erickson, M.D.* 3 vols. New York: Triangle, 1985.

Hersen, M., and Barlow, D. *Single Case Experimental Designs: Strategies for Studying Behavior Change.* New York: Pergamon Press, 1976.

Hsai, H. "Structural and Strategic Approach to School Phobia/School Refusal." *Psychology in the Schools,* 1984, *24,* 145–152.

Keeney, B., and Ross, J. *Mind in Therapy: Constructing Systemic Family Therapies.* New York: Basic Books, 1985.

Keller, H. "Behavioral Consultation." In J. Conoley (ed.), *Consultation in Schools.* New York: Academic Press, 1981.

Kiresuk, T., and Sherman, R. "Goal Attainment Scaling: A General Method for Evaluating Comprehensive Mental Health Programs." *Community Mental Health,* 1968, *4,* 443–453.

Kral, R. "Indirect Therapy in the Schools." In S. DeShazer and R. Kral (eds.), *Indirect Approaches in Therapy*. Rockville, Md.: Aspen, 1986.

Lindquist, B., Molnar, A., and Brauchman, L. "Working with School-Related Problems Without Going to School." *Journal of Strategic and Systemic Therapies*, 1987, *6*, 44–50.

Madanes, C. *Strategic Family Therapy*. San Francisco: Jossey-Bass, 1981.

Maruyama, M. "The Second Cybernetics: Deviation-Amplifying Mutual Causative Processes." *American Scientist*, 1963, *51*, 164–179.

Minuchin, S. *Families and Family Therapy*. Cambridge, Mass.: Harvard University Press, 1974.

Nelsen, J. "Issues in Single-Subject Research for Non-Behaviorists." *Social Work Research and Abstracts*, 1981, *31*, 31–37.

O'Connor, J. "Why Can't I Get Hives: Brief Strategic Therapy with an Obsessional Child." *Family Process*, 1983, *22*, 201–209.

O'Hanlon, W. *Taproots: Underlying Principles of Milton Erickson's Therapy and Hypnosis*. New York: Norton, 1987.

O'Shea, M., and Jessee, E. "Ethical, Value and Professional Conflicts in Systems Therapy." In J. Hansen and L. L'Abate (eds.), *Values, Ethics, Legalities and the Family Therapist*. Rockville, Md.: Aspen, 1982.

Papp, P. *The Process of Change*. New York: Guilford, 1983.

Parsonson, B., and Baer, D. "The Analyses and Presentation of Graphed Data." In T. R. Kratochwill (ed.), *Single Subject Research: Strategies for Evaluating Change*. New York: Academic Press, 1978.

Power, T., and Bartholomew, K. "Getting Uncaught in the Middle: A Case Study in Family-School System Consultation." *School Psychology Review*, 1988, *17*, 213–214.

Rosenthal, M., and Bergman, Z. "The Decision-Making Process of the MRI Brief Therapy Center." *Journal of Strategic and Systemic Therapies*, 1986, *5* (1), 11–16.

Saposnek, D. "Aikido: A Model for Brief Strategic Therapy." *Family Process*, 1980, *19* (3), 227–238.

Segal, L. "Brief Family Therapy." In A. Horne and M. Ohlsen (eds.), *Family Counseling and Therapy*. Itasca, Ill.: Peacock, 1982.

Selvini-Palazolli, M., Boscolo, L., Cecchin, G., and Prata, G. *Paradox and Counterparadox*. New York: Jason Aronson, 1978.

Watzlawick, P., Weakland, J., and Fisch, R. *Change: Principles of Problem Formation and Problem Resolution*. New York: Norton, 1974.

Weakland, J. H. "Family Somatics—A Neglected Edge." *Family Process*, 1977a, *16* (3), 263–272.

Weakland, J. H. "OK—You've Been a Bad Mother." In P. Papp (ed.), *Family Therapy Full Length Case Studies*. New York: Gardner, 1977b.

Weakland, J. H., Fisch, R., Watzlawick, R., and Bodin, A. "Brief Therapy: Focused Problem Resolution." *Family Process*, 1974, *13* (2), 141–168.

Wender, P. "Vicious and Virtuous Cycles: The Role of Deviation Amplifying Feedback in the Origin and Perpetuation of Behavior." *Psychiatry: Journal for the Study of Interpersonal Processes*, 1968, *31* (4), 309–324.

Wetchler, J. "Family Therapy of School-Focused Problems: A Macrosystemic Perspective." *Contemporary Family Therapy*, 1986, *8* (3), 224–241.

Williams, J., and Weeks, G. "Use of Paradoxical Techniques in the School Setting." *American Journal of Family Therapy*, 1984, *12*, 47–59.

Wiswell, J. "Homework Difficulties Resolved by Counselor's Intervention." *American Association for Counseling and Development (AACD) Guidepost*, 1986, *29* (24), 7.

Zarske, J. A. "The Treatment of Temper Tantrums in a Cerebral Palsied Child: A Paradoxical Intervention." *School Psychology Review*, 1982, *11*, 324–328.

INDEX

Academic underachievement, brief strategic intervention for, 32-34, 36-37

Accountability, and monitoring, 130-131

Ackerman Institute, 36

Acting out, beliefs about, 94-96

Amatea, E., 6, 55n, 103n, 151n

Anderson, A., 190-191

Anderson, H., 23

Assignments, planning intervention for, 104-106, 111, 112

Attributions, reframing, 126-127

Avoidance: and solution thrust, 112-116; and strategic shift, 117-120

B

Bad language, information gathering on, 86-87

Baer, D., 144

Barlow, D., 131, 132, 133, 137, 141, 143, 144

Bartholomew, K., 134

Becky, 151-164

Behavioral therapy, brief strategic intervention compared with, 15, 16, 21

Beliefs: agreement and shift for, 96; assessing, 94-102; and benevolent frame, 163; and coercive and avoidance solution thrusts, 114-115; about control, 99-100; importance of, 95; and motivation, 100-101; 112; about problem, 97-99; and reframing, 19, 99-101, 125-126, 163; and strategic shift, 120; on urgency and difficulty, 98; using, 99-101

Belittling, information gathering on, 88

Bergman, Z., 61, 89

Bobby, 57-58

Bodin, A., 6, 16, 79, 135-137

Bowen, M., 34

Brauchman, L., 107

Brief strategic intervention: advantages of, 192-193; as alternative therapy, 3-21; analysis of, 1-41; appropriate conditions for, 47, 191-192; assumptions in, 7-8; basis of, 1-2; beliefs assessed and used in, 94-102; change process in, 55-77; comparisons with, 15; deciding to use, 45-54; information gathering in, 78-93; monitoring and evaluating, 129-148; planning and implementing, 103-128; practice of, 43-148; premises of, 22-41; reactions to, 189-191; responsible use of, 189-193; as school-focused, 18, 192-193; steps in, 9-14, 37-38; for stu-

Brief strategic intervention
(continued)
dent problems, 149–193. *See also*
Interventions
Bullying, behavioral therapy for, 16

C

Carrow, P., 149, 179
Carter, Mrs., 152–154, 158
Causation, cybernetic paradigm of, 26
Change process: aspects of managing, 55–77; barriers to, 46–47; identifying initial terms for, 56–58; involvement in, 17–18, 58–59, 62–64, 68–74; and limitations of initial terms, 58–59; monitoring, 13–14, 129–148; redefining initial terms in, 59–60; testing and confirming, 112
Clients: beliefs of, 94–102; in interactional whole, 23; undermining position of, 66–68, 72–74
Coercion: and solution thrust, 112–116; and strategic shift, 117–120
Compliance through voluntarism pattern, in problem behavior, 51–52
Confidentiality, issue of, 190
Conflict: brief strategic intervention for, 38–41; pattern of, in problem behavior, 50–51, 180–184
Connie, 122–126
Control: beliefs about, 99–100; and reframing, 54
Crying, extending ideas about, 61–64

D

D., Mr. and Mrs., 166–178
Debbie, 85–86
Defending pattern, in problem behavior, 52–53
DeShazer, S., 34
Distracting others, information gathering on, 85–86
Distress, short-term, 191

E

Erickson, M., 19, 120, 126, 127
Evaluation. *See* Monitoring

F

Family systems therapy, brief strategic intervention compared with, 6, 15, 17, 21
Fear and postponement pattern, in problem behavior, 49–50, 117, 120–121
Fisch, R., 1, 6, 16, 28, 29, 30, 34, 35, 40n, 47, 49, 50, 51, 52, 53, 66, 68, 69, 79, 84, 89, 91, 112, 113, 115n, 117, 119n, 120–121, 122, 126, 127, 134, 135–136
Fisher, L., 190–191
Folsom, Mrs., 3–4, 9, 13
Forcing pattern, in problem behavior, 48–49, 54
Fragility, and indirectness, 52

G

G., Mrs., 165–166, 177–178
George, 104–106, 111, 112
Goal-attainment scaling, in monitoring, 138, 141
Goolishan, H., 23
Greene, Mrs., 88
Greg, 81, 83

H

Haley, J., 17, 126, 190
Hayes, S., 131, 132, 137, 141, 143
Hersen, M., 132, 133, 144
Homework, monitoring intervention for, 138, 141, 142, 144, 145–148
Hsai, H., 134–135

I

Implementation: and intervention planning, 121–128; reframing for, 11–13, 123–128